Stephanie Arsenault

111 Places in San Diego That You Must Not Miss

emons:

To me.

Nice work, babe! *high-fives self*

Cäcilienstraße 48, 50667 Köln
info@emons-verlag.de

Cover icons: shutterstock/Nganhaycuoi; Karolin Meinert
Cover layout: Karolin Meinert
Design: Eva Kraskes, based on a design
by Lübbeke | Naumann | Thoben
Maps: altancicek.design, www.altancicek.de
Basic cartographical information from Openstreetmap,
© OpenStreetMap-Mitwirkende, OdbL
Edited by: Karen E. Seiger
Printing and binding: Grafisches Centrum Cuno, Calbe
Printed in Germany 2025
ISBN 978-3-7408-1540-0
First edition

Guidebooks for Locals & Experienced Travellers
Join us in uncovering new places around the world at
www.111places.com

Foreword

I first traveled to San Diego back in 2013 when my husband was attending a conference, and I tagged along. While he was busy with work colleagues, I explored the city, popping into restaurants and breweries for a quick bite and a pint, wandering through the beauty that is Balboa Park, and splashing in the waves at Pacific Beach. Together, we visited the USS *Midway*, ogled the animals at the zoo, and rode the roller coaster on repeat at Belmont Park.

We fell in love with the city, came back several times, and eventually found ourselves living here, drawn to the constant sunshine, gentle sway of the tall palms, and the laid-back vibe of SoCal. Coming from Alberta, Canada, there have been plenty of "We're not in Kansas anymore" moments, and while Calgary will always be home, San Diego is also a place we are honored to call home too. It's beautiful, welcoming, and seems to have been made for adventure.

As a transplant, I feel like I've ventured out more than many people who have lived here all their lives. It's easy to get used to things and take them for granted while they're right in front of you, but for a newbie, it's only natural to want to see everything a new place offers. In the years since we've moved here, I've done my best to explore every corner of this picturesque county not as a tourist, but as a local with fresh eyes.

Finding 111 unique, special places in San Diego to share was not a challenge – there are countless cool spots here. The challenge was narrowing it down and picking what seems like a handful of gems that need to be shared. Of course, I couldn't include everything, but I tried to do San Diego justice, and I hope you agree that I have. Thank you for picking up this book, and for exploring San Diego with me. I can't wait to share this adventure with you, with sand between our toes, sun on our skin, and our minds open to all that this gorgeous place has to offer.

111 Places

1 Aero Club Bar

Celebrating aviation one whiskey at a time

In 1947, a local pilot opened the Aero Club Bar, and the establishment has been a mainstay in San Diego's bar scene for nearly 80 years. Marianne Profit, the founding pilot, was herself a rarity, as it was very uncommon for women to become pilots at that time.

Aero Club is best known as a cool dive bar near the airport, but the history behind it is what truly keeps it special. Profit wanted a place near the airport where she and her fellow pilots, airline staff, and workers from a nearby aircraft factory could relax and enjoy a drink. The bar, which quickly became a popular spot for the aviation community, has remained in the perfect location for those on their way to or from the airport, and is now considered to be one of San Diego's best dive bars.

In the beginning, the bar's ambiance was carefully crafted to celebrate aviation, with décor featuring airplane models, old pilot uniforms, and aviation memorabilia. Over the decades, the Aero Club Bar has retained much of its original charm and features, and the vintage feel of the bar makes it possible to imagine just what it would have looked like when Profit first opened the doors.

Despite changes in ownership and management, the joint has steadfastly preserved its historical essence while evolving to cater to modern tastes, notably illustrated by the assortment of pinball, arcade, and table games, plus the epic mural painted by local artist Brian "HEBS" Hebets, featuring Godzilla versus WWII-era and modern fighter jets. One of the best features of current-day Aero Club is its huge whiskey collection. With over 1,200 different varieties available, it has become a renowned destination for whiskey enthusiasts in and around the city. There are also over 20 craft brews on tap and a food truck on their cozy patio. Amidst the nostalgia, fun, and tasty options available, you're bound to have a good time.

Address 3365 India Street, San Diego, CA 92103, +1 (619) 297-7211, www.aeroclubbar.com | Getting there Trolley to Middletown (Blue or Green Lines) | Hours Mon–Thu 2pm–2am, Fri–Sun noon–2am | Tip Experience another epic and historic dive bar at Waterfront Bar & Grill in Little Italy (2044 Kettner Boulevard, www.waterfrontbarandgrill.com).

2 Annie's Canyon

A hidden natural wonder

Annie's Canyon Loop Trail, often referred to by locals as Mushroom Caves or just Annie's Canyon, is situated within the gorgeous landscape of the San Elijo Lagoon Ecological Reserve in Solana Beach. This reserve, one of San Diego's largest wetlands, sets the stage for a unique hiking experience that blends coastal beauty with geological wonder.

The trailhead marks the beginning of a 2.3-mile loop that takes hikers along the lagoon. The pathway meanders through coastal sage scrub, mixed chaparral, and many other stunning plants, creating a picturesque setting that attracts both nature enthusiasts and avid birdwatchers. Be sure to bring your binoculars to get a good look at some of the local fowl.

While you're following the trail, also keep your eyes peeled for deer, lizards, snakes, and other residents of the reserve.

At the end of the trail / beginning of the canyon, the narrow sandstone walls greet visitors with a promise of an otherworldly experience. It's important for you to understand before you set out that the canyon's tight squeezes might not be suitable for anyone prone to claustrophobia. The hike presents a mix of terrains, ladder-style stairs, switchback paths, and spots that require some scrambling. So exercise caution, especially in sections where erosion may pose a threat, and keep your comfort levels in mind.

Your efforts, however, will be rewarded with breathtaking vistas of the Pacific and the lagoon. The trail is a treasure trove of natural wonders.

It's worth noting that this trail, which was once off-limits, has become a beloved and legally accessible gem. While technically dog-friendly, certain sections, such as those with ladders, are not ideal for canine companions. As such, it's better to leave your four-legged friends at home so you can fully enjoy the unique experience and challenges that Annie's Canyon has to offer.

Address 126 Solana Point Circle, Solana Beach, CA 92075 | Getting there Coaster or Pacific Surfliner to Solana Beach; bus 101 to Highway 101 & Cliff Street | Hours Daily dawn–dusk | Tip Visit the San Elijo Lagoon Nature Center for stunning views of the area from their second-floor observation deck, and learn all about the ecological reserve via interactive exhibits (2710 Manchester Avenue, Cardiff-by-the-Sea, www.naturecollective.org).

3 Barona Cultural Center & Museum

Exploring Kumeyaay heritage

Kumeyaay (pronounced, koo-mee-eye) people are the original inhabitants of San Diego County, long before the expedition of Juan Rodriguez Cabrillo (1497–1543), and long, long before surfing and tacos became part of San Diego's identity. The Barona Cultural Center & Museum dedicated to preserving and understanding the history and culture of Kumeyaay heritage is located on the Barona Band of Mission Indians Reservation and offers an in-depth view of 10,000 years of local history.

The museum's collection includes everyday and ceremonial items demonstrating the artistry and craftsmanship of the Kumeyaay people, such as coiled baskets, grinding stones, and pottery, as well as ancient stone tools and shell objects. There are also interactive exhibits, maps of ancient territories, and displays that illustrate essential aspects of Kumeyaay life, their knowledge of plants, and traditional practices like basketry.

You will learn about the impact of colonization on the Kumeyaay, including three significant waves of newcomers over the past 250 years, from the Kumeyaay perspective, emphasizing their experiences and struggles during these changes, especially the near loss of their culture and language during this period, and the efforts underway today to revitalize and preserve these traditions.

The museum features the award-winning film *Nya'waap Illyuw Uuchyuwp – Our Way of Knowing*, which shares the Kumeyaay Creation Story. This movie, alongside exhibits on traditional practices, provides a deeper understanding of their worldview and spiritual beliefs. There's also a research library with over a thousand books and rare volumes, and an archive of photographs and documents available to visitors seeking a deeper dive into Kumeyaay history and culture.

Address 1095 Barona Road, Lakeside, CA 92040, +1 (619) 443-7003, ext. 219, www.baronamuseum.com, museum@baronamuseum.org | Getting there By car, from Lakeside, head north on Ashwood Street, continue onto Wildcat Canyon Road for 6 miles, pass the entry to the casino, and continue toward the Barona Community Center. The museum is on the left, within the Community Center. | Hours Thu & Fri noon – 5pm, Sat 10am – 4pm | Tip If you find your belly rumbling after an afternoon at the museum, head to Grand Ole BBQ Flinn Springs for some Central Texas-style meats smoked on a BBQ pit hand-built in Georgia (15505 Olde Highway 80, El Cajon, flinnsprings.grandolebbq.com).

4 Barrio Glassworks

It's a beautiful day in the neighborhood

Located in the laid-back neighborhood of Barrio in Carlsbad, Barrio Glassworks is both a gallery and a studio. It's a space where visitors get to check out artists hard at work or, if they're feeling brave, can try their hand at the ancient art themselves. It's a place where local and resident artists can come in and explore their art, while feeling supported by the community (which, appropriately, is what Barrio translates to: community/neighborhood).

The studio and gallery are owned by Mary Devlin and Gary Raskin, who were introduced to glassblowing by their son, Drew (who is the studio manager). All three have a background in and passion for the craft, and are eager to share their love and knowledge with visitors.

The art of glassblowing itself was invented by Syrian craftsmen between 27 BC and 14 AD, and the techniques have been perfected over the centuries. That said, artists are constantly working on unique ways to create new, beautiful designs. The rotating exhibitions at Barrio Glassworks show off work from local and international artists, offering a look into the craft, and inspiration for those who want to give it a shot!

During the Make Your Own hands-on glass experience, visitors are guided by team members from Barrio Glassworks to make their own unique objects, like glass paperweights. Creating something out of glass is no easy feat, and it's a very hot one – the transformation of materials into glass happens at around 2,400 degrees Fahrenheit, then the temperature is reduced to around 2,000 degrees, which is the working temperature. It typically takes a couple of days for the glass to fully cool, a process called annealing.

Once they've completed the Make Your Own experience, participants can take private lessons and learn how to make more complicated items like bowls, vases, or cups – creating new glass artists one class at a time!

Address 3060 Roosevelt Street, Carlsbad, CA 92008, +1 (760) 696-3288, www.barrioglassworks.com, info@barrioglassworks.com | Getting there Coaster to Carlsbad Village; bus 315 or 325 to Grand Avenue & Roosevelt Street or Carlsbad Village | Hours Visit website for up-to-date hours; classes by appointment only | Tip Learn another, more low-key craft in knitting or crocheting, or just stock up on supplies at Apricot Yarn & Supply (2690 Historic Decatur Road, No. 101, www.apricotyarn.com).

5 Belly Up

A historical SoCal live-music venue

Sitting in the middle of Solana Beach's Design District on Cedros Avenue is Belly Up, a music venue that offers the perfect blend of live music and the classic Southern California-esque, relaxed, beach vibe. Since 1974, this cozy, intimate spot has hosted an exceptional variety of artists, from world-renowned bands, to local cover groups, and everything in between.

Despite huge names like Etta James, Death Cab for Cutie, and B.B. King making their way to the stage, this is no huge stadium. It's situated in a fancy strip mall full of upscale clothing boutiques and design studios, and holds only around 600 fans.

The biggest benefit of the small space is that Belly Up ends up being the kind of place where you're up close with the artists, so it feels more like a jam session with friends than a typical concert. A jam session with people like Willie Nelson, Childish Gambino, and Mick Jagger. Yes, Mick Jagger graced this small-town stage, but you'd never know that it's such a big deal just by looking at it. The people who run the place also know how to keep things exciting with random, unexpected performances by well-known musicians like Eddie Vedder.

For the ultimate Belly Up experience, make a reservation at Tavern, the attached restaurant, before the show. If you grab dinner there, you'll also get access to the venue's side door and will have a much shorter wait to get in. Patrons can also enjoy the full bar and tasty, pub-style bites in Belly Up that are served up from Tavern's kitchen. Pro tip (but you might want to keep this to yourself): if you can go early, snag a seat to the right of the stage for great, unobstructed views and table service.

So next time checking out live music is on your to-do list, make sure Belly Up is the first place you look; after all, you never know who you'll stumble upon in this coastal town's historical spot.

Address 143 S Cedros Avenue, Solana Beach, CA 92075, +1 (858) 481-8140, www.bellyup.com, boxoffice@bellyup.com | Getting there Coaster or Pacific Surfliner to Solana Beach; bus 101 to Highway 101 & Plaza Street | Hours See website for schedule; box office Sat–Thu 4pm–close, Fri noon–close | Tip Sip on a pint of award-winning craft beer right from the source at Culture Brewing down the street (S Cedros Avenue, www.culturebrewingco.com).

6 Bo's Boots on Wheels

It's time for some new boot goofin'

Established in 2005 as Sin City Skates, this shop, now called Bo's Boots on Wheels, is a different kind of SoCal skate shop. In a place where surf and skate (of the skateboard variety) shops are at every corner, Bo's is like the cool, unassuming little sister who will kick your butt, given the chance. Sure, they sell roller skates fit for Barbie and Ken on the boardwalk, but they're also all about roller derby.

Back in 2005 when Sin City Skates first opened, it was the first store ever dedicated to roller derby. Founded by Ivanna S. Pankin and Trish the Dish, the shop became a lifeline for derby skaters near and far. In 2017, Kelly "Bo Toxic" Timm, a San Diego native and longtime derby skater, took over. Under her leadership, the shop expanded to cater to all kinds of skaters, while staying true to its derby beginnings.

Roller derby, if you're unfamiliar, is an intense and exciting sport where teams score points by helping their "jammers" lap the opposing team, and they do it all on roller skates. It's a mix of strategy, speed, and physicality. And it's as inclusive as it gets, often with a bit of a feminist/punk vibe. The sport embraces all genders, body types, and skill levels, and many leagues are skater-run. Here in San Diego, there are two teams: the San Diego Derby United, and North County's Hidden City Roller Derby.

With derby and recreational skating in mind, Bo's offers just about everything a skater could need: roller skates, inline skates, safety gear, and all the accessories. If you're dreaming of building custom skates, they can help with that too, letting you mix and match components to create your perfect pair, or even make you a pair out of your favorite sneakers. Staff members are all experienced skaters themselves, so they know their stuff and can help you figure out exactly what you need, whether you're new to skating or a seasoned pro.

Address 8280 Clairemont Mesa Boulevard, No. 126, San Diego, CA 92111, +1 (619) 232-4200, www.bosbootsonwheels.com, info@sincityskates.com | **Getting there** Bus 43 or 44 to Clairemont Mesa Boulevard & Industrial Park | **Hours** Tue–Fri noon–6pm, Sat & Sun 11am–5pm | **Tip** Head to the Salty Garage shop, tucked behind Salt Culture in Encinitas, to check out surf legend Rob Machado's surfboards. All boards are designed by Machado himself, and many shaped by him as well (932 S Coast Highway 101, Encinitas, www.rmsurfboards.com).

7 Bompensiero Mob Hit

Where an informant met his fate

Frank Bompensiero (1905–1977), also known as "Bomp," was a prominent figure in the Southern California Mafia, particularly within the Los Angeles crime family. He was born in Milwaukee, Wisconsin to a Sicilian family that had immigrated to the US the year before. Bompensiero moved to San Diego in the 1920s and was known for his role in typical Mafia activities like gambling, booze smuggling, loan sharking, and extortion, earning him a reputation as a respected and feared mobster.

Notably, Bompensiero was deeply involved in the Mafia's operations as a hitman, a role for which he was known for his ruthlessness and effectiveness. In fact, one of his associates, Jimmy Fratianno, once said that he "had buried more bones than could be found in the Brontosaurus room of the Museum of Natural History."

His life, however, took a significant turn when he began cooperating with the FBI as a confidential informant (CI). This collaboration with law enforcement started at least a decade before his death, and as he was getting on the nerves of other Mafia members in Southern California. So this new role was a major betrayal in the eyes of the crime family and eventually made him a target within the criminal underworld.

Despite being a CI, Bompensiero managed to keep up appearances within the Mafia, which allowed him to provide the FBI with valuable information. His insights into their operations, key figures, and internal dynamics were crucial in the FBI's efforts to combat organized crime.

This double life, however, led to his demise. In 1977, Bompensiero was assassinated in Pacific Beach, a hit believed to have been orchestrated by his Mafia associates who had uncovered his role as a CI. Bompensiero was walking back from the pay phone outside the ARCO station near his home when the hit happened, an apparent kill in return for the shooter's membership into the LA family.

Address 1875 Grand Avenue, San Diego, CA 92109 | Getting there Bus 30 to Grand Avenue & Lamont Street. The crime occurred just a few yards south of the ARCO station on Lamont Street. | Hours Unrestricted | Tip Venture further west to Crystal Pier and check out incredible views of Pacific Beach, or stay in one of the cozy historic cottages atop the pier (4500 Ocean Boulevard, www.crystalpier.com).

8 *Breaking of the Chains*

A reminder of the past as a lesson for the future

In the midst of the always-bustling Gaslamp District is the *Breaking of the Chains* monument. Unveiled in 1995, this enormous sculpture is crafted from polished stainless steel and serves as a tribute to the spirit of the Civil Rights Movement and the continuous struggle for racial justice and equality.

The mind behind the piece is artist Melvin Edwards. Born in 1937 in Houston, Texas, Edwards is a celebrated figure in the history of Black art, known for his ability to intertwine themes of racial injustice into his work. His dedication to addressing social issues through art has left an indelible mark on this masterpiece, and it goes beyond the realm of sculpture, evolving into a visual narrative set against the Martin Luther King Jr. Promenade.

Breaking of the Chains exudes the profound wisdom of Dr. King, particularly his emphasis on love and morality as instrumental in breaking the metaphorical chains of hate and discrimination. The sculpture's polished stainless-steel form is an indisputable representation of the unyielding strength of those who have fought and continue to advocate for equality.

Visitors are invited to reflect on the impactful teachings of Dr. King, and the true meaning of the work he did. To help prompt this reflection, the monument also features a plaque with a quote by Dr. King that says, "Along the way of life, someone must have the sense enough, and morality enough, to cut off the chain of hate. This can only be done by projecting the ethic of love to the center of our lives."

Edwards' creation honors the past bravery against injustice while hoping to inspire future activism, offering a chance for reflection about the role each individual plays in the pursuit of justice, and playing a crucial role in understanding the depth of both the Civil Rights Movement and the legacy of Dr. Martin Luther King Jr.

Address 301 1st Avenue, San Diego, CA 92101 | **Getting there** Trolley to Gaslamp Quarter or Seaport Village (Green or Silver Lines); bus 280, 290, 923 or 992 to Broadway & Pacific Highway | **Hours** Unrestricted | **Tip** Learn all about African American, African Spanish, and African Mexican heritage at the African Diaspora Museum and Research Center (2471 Congress Street, www.africanmuseumsandiego.com).

9 Buena Vista Lagoon

Preserving nature's quiet refuge on the coast

Tucked right between the cities of Oceanside and Carlsbad is the Buena Vista Lagoon Ecological Reserve, a rare, freshwater, coastal wetland that spans over 220 acres. This stunning expanse of open water, dense reeds, and native vegetation offers a glimpse into an ecosystem thriving against the backdrop of urban sprawl. It's a place where nature exists quietly, noticed only through the ripples of a hidden fish, the sharp call of a heron in flight, or the slow glide of a grebe across glassy water.

Established in 1968 as California's very first ecological reserve, Buena Vista Lagoon is a sanctuary for over 200 species of birds, including the elusive and light-footed Ridgway's rail and the delicate Belding's Savannah sparrow, both endangered and deeply reliant on the lagoon's unique habitat. Birdwatchers come here with patience and binoculars, hoping to catch sight of these rare inhabitants, while photographers linger along the water's edge, waiting for golden hour and its picture-perfect light to illuminate the marsh.

Over the years, sediment buildup, invasive plant species, and debates over freshwater versus saltwater restoration have kept the reserve at the center of conservation discussions. Advocates argue over the best path forward, all while the lagoon continues its quiet work or filtering water, sheltering life, and offering a refuge to those who pause long enough to notice.

Adjacent to the reserve, the Buena Vista Audubon Society Nature Center has exhibits that dive into the lagoon's ecology, while volunteers lead walks along shaded paths where native plants like pickleweed and cordgrass thrive.

Despite the hum of nearby highways (it's right between the 101 and 5) and the outlines of homes on the horizon, Buena Vista Lagoon is a timeless pocket of wilderness. It's the perfect spot to take a walk, look for birds, or just exist while taking it all in.

Address 2202 S Coast Highway, Oceanside, CA 92054, +1 (619) 439-2473, www.bvaudubon.org | Getting there Bus 101 to Coast Highway & Eaton Street | Hours Nature Center Tue–Sat 10am–1pm; trail: daily dawn–dusk | Tip For another bird-filled (but with decidedly more eggs) experience, head to Happy Hens for a day at the farm, while learning about the pasture-raised birds and humane practices utilized here (2176 Ramona Street, Ramona, www.happy-hens.com).

10 Bum the Dog

A tribute to the city's best friend

There are few tails… er… tales (sorry) better than those of a beloved dog, and San Diego has not just one, but two commemorative statues of cherished pups. Behold: Bum the Dog, and his buddy, Bobby (they weren't actually friends, but surely they are in the afterlife because they were such good boys). Bobby was a loyal terrier owned by a policeman in Edinburgh, Scotland. He was so loyal that he even spent years at his owner's grave after the officer had passed; so, while he and Bum didn't pal around in life, Bobby deserves a shout-out, too.

Bum is the one and only official dog of San Diego. Born to a stray in San Francisco in 1886, Bum was initially taken in by a fire department. He quickly realized, however, that he was much too independent to stay in one place and decided a life of adventure, and often luxury, was more his style. So, Bum hopped on the *Santa Rosa*, a steamship bound for San Diego, and wandered the town, figuring out his new life. He was given shelter and food, and rubbed shoulders with local aristocrats. One restaurant even posted a sign saying, "Bum eats here" – what an endorsement!

In 1891, San Diego passed a law that required all dogs to be registered, and the city gave Bum a tag for life, with his image being stamped on all licenses that were issued. Later in life, Bum developed rheumatism, and the San Diego Board of Supervisors ordered that he retire in the County Hospital – and that's where Bum passed on, in 1896, at the age of 12.

The bronze statues of Bum and Bobby, made by California-born artist Jessica McCain, were unveiled in 2007, and sit in the pocket park at the Gaslamp Museum at the Davis-Horton House. Identical statues are on display near Greyfriars Church in Edinburgh, representing the connection between the two cities (who've been sister cities since 1977) and the shared experiences and loyalty of the two dogs.

Address 401 Island Avenue, San Diego, CA 92101, www.gaslampfoundation.org/bum-the-dog | Getting there Trolley to Convention Center (Green or Silver Lines); bus 3 to Market Street & 6th Avenue or 4th Avenue & G Street | Hours Unrestricted | Tip Celebrate man's best friend with a trip to Fiesta Island, a big island within Mission Bay, where pups have free rein and owners can enjoy the fire pits, picnic spots, and seemingly endless beaches (1590 E Mission Bay Drive).

11 Cabrillo Tidepools

Take a look at what's under the sea

The Cabrillo Tidepools, located within the Cabrillo National Monument and Cabrillo State Marine Reserve, offer a unique look into a dynamic ecosystem. This Rocky Intertidal Zone, where the ocean meets the land, endures significant changes in temperature, weather, and surf, which helps to explain why so many cool creatures live here.

For the best experience, plan your visit by first checking sites like www.tide-forecast.com for up-to-date tide schedules. Aim to arrive just before low tide because you'll be able to see more tidepools and diverse marine life. While the tidepools are accessible year-round, winter months offer the most dramatic low tides. There is a fee to enter the park, though parking is free once you're inside.

During low tide, you can see an array of marine life, including limpets, crabs, marine snails, sea stars, anemones, California sea hares, sea lettuce, moray eels, sea urchins, nudibranchs, spiny lobsters, and occasionally even octopuses! This ecosystem is delicate, so do not handle organisms or disturb their habitats. Stick to designated paths, wear sturdy shoes, and watch your step to avoid harming the environment and yourself, as the algae covering many of the rocks is slippery.

Once you're done checking out the inhabitants of the tidepools, the high cliffs at Point Loma make it a great spot for whale watching. The volunteers stationed near the parking lot are quick to let you know what kinds of marine life you're likely to see during your visit.

It's important to note that Point Loma itself has an extremely rich history. It was established in 1797 as an artillery station, and it's been used by the US military since 1852. The Cabrillo National Monument marks the landing of Juan Rodríguez Cabrillo (ca. 1497–1543) at San Diego Bay in 1542 during the first European expedition on the West Coast of what would become the United States.

Address Lands End Road, San Diego, CA 92016, +1 (619) 557-5450, www.nps.gov/cabr | **Getting there** By car, take Route 5 to exit 18A to Pacific Highway. Keep left onto Barnett Avenue, and turn left onto Catalina Boulevard to the Cabrillo National Monument Fee Entry Booth. Continue on Cabrillo Road, keep left into the parking lot, and the tidepools are on the southwest corner. | **Hours** Daily 9am–4:30pm | **Tip** Book a dinner reservation at the glamorous Marine Room during high tide, and you'll feel like you're under the sea as the waves crash against the restaurant's windows (1950 Spindrift Drive, La Jolla, www.marineroom.com).

12 Calcite Mine Slot Canyon

A literal hidden gem

What do you get when you mix nature and science, add a pinch of history, and stir in a smattering of gorgeous views? The Calcite Mine Slot Canyon hike in Anza-Borrego Desert State Park, that's what. This nearly four-mile-round-trip hike winds through narrow slot canyons with towering, smooth rock walls, and a calcite mine from the mid-20th century.

The mine itself is not obviously visible. Instead, you'll first see remnants of the mining operation, including trenches, discarded rock piles, and bits of calcite, offering a glimpse into the mining techniques of the era. So, why calcite? This mineral, composed of calcium carbonate and formed in the sedimentary rock layers over millions of years, has optical clarity and double refraction properties that made it valuable for wartime optical devices.

During World War II, there was a high demand for calcite, as it was used in precision instruments like gun sights and bomb sights. This mine is the only one of its kind in the US and was established in the early 1940s. It played a crucial role in meeting this demand, and miners had to use hand tools to remove the calcite crystals carefully from the rock formations.

The mine site is accessible via a short hike from the end of Calcite Mine Road, a dirt road accessible to high-clearance vehicles (regular vehicles can park at the junction with Highway 78, adding an extra mile to the trek). You can explore the mine trenches and surrounding areas, but exercise caution and respect the fragile desert environment.

The best time to visit is from late fall to early spring to avoid the extreme desert heat, but regardless of the time of year, be sure to bring plenty of water, snacks, and sun protection, as there are no services along or near the trail. It's also a good idea to download a map of the area so you'll have it offline just in case you get off track.

Address Calcite Road, Borrego Springs, CA 92004 | Getting there By car, from the Anza Borrego Visitor's Center, head south on Stirrup Road toward Palm Canyon Drive, turn left at the first cross street onto Palm Canyon Drive to Pegleg Road, and then continue onto Borrego Salton Sea Way for just over 12 miles. The trailhead will be on the left. | Hours Unrestricted | Tip Head west on Borrego Salton Seaway for an incredible view of the area, including the Salton Sea, from the Badlands Viewpoint (Calcite Road, three minutes west of Calcite Mine Slot Canyon Trailhead).

13 Calico Cidery

A taste of liquid gold

If you stop by Calico Cidery, you're bound to be greeted by a couple of friendly taproom folks, a happy farm pup, and an orchard that's been growing apples and pears since the 1920s. In fact, the ranch boasts pear trees over 100 years old that still bear fruit! Back in the 1980s, mechanical engineer Conrad Young purchased the ranch and revitalized the orchard, and recently, Young's son David, a pomology graduate from Cal Poly and a winemaker, joined his dad in refocusing the orchard towards cider making.

Calico is best known for producing their extremely delicious ciders, but much of their work goes into maintaining the ranch's historical roots, including nearly 100 apple varieties, with an extensive specimen orchard planted by Conrad. Standout varieties include Winesap, a Southern apple great for both eating and single-varietal cider; Calville Blanc, a French apple that adds body to cider blends; and Wickson crab-apples, a small, tangy apple with a tropical punch flavor. The Conrads also grow quince, which adds unique aromatics and astringency to some ciders.

Of course, making cider is a group effort. Calico's cider maker, Ian Wright, was initially brought in to run the taproom, but he quickly moved to the production end due to his winemaking background. He's the man behind the delectable, co-fermented apples, pears, and other fruit that go into creating unique and dynamic ciders.

Now, for the *pièce de résistance*: The tasting room. It's tucked inside a barn and outfitted with an antique bar from the 1880s (sourced from the East Coast), farm tables, and hay bales draped in plaid blankets, making it the perfect, rustic spot for an afternoon sip. In the summer, the shade of the barn provides relief from the sun. During the cooler months, heaters warm the space, outdoor fireplaces add to the cozy aesthetic, and the hot mulled cider alone makes the trip worthwhile.

Address 4200 Highway 78, Julian, CA 92036, +1 (858) 585-0392, www.calicocidery.com | Getting there By car, drive CA-78 toward Calico Ranch Road. The cidery is on the east side of the highway. | Hours Thu–Mon 11am–6pm | Tip Try the best darn sangria out there at the Blue Door Winery in Julian; it's made fresh, and you can even get a bottle of it to go (2608 B Street, Julian, www.thebluedoorwinery.com).

14 The California Surf Museum

Riding the waves of history

Aptly located just down the street from the pier and the beach in Oceanside, the California Surf Museum (CSM) offers a deep dive into the rich history and vibrant culture of surfing. Since its conception 1986, this museum has been an interactive, informative space that shows off everything from the Polynesian origins of surfing to its modern-day iterations.

With an impressive collection of surf-related items, the exhibits here are beautifully curated. There's an array of vintage surfboards that chronicle the technological advancements and design innovations that have transformed surfing over the decades. In addition to the surfboards, you'll also find memorabilia, photographs, and film footage that capture crucial moments in surf history, including the display of what one could call the OG GoPro.

CSM has created a rare and valuable collection. For nearly 40 years, the staff has gathered archives and artifacts, creating one of the richest troves of surfing history. This collection is a draw for researchers and historians, but also for fans of the sport, offering a look into the surfing world. There's also a dedicated space for special exhibitions, which rotate throughout the year. These showcases focus on a variety of themes, such as the contributions of pioneering surfers like La Jolla's Woody Ekstrom (1927–2022), surfing competitions, the science of waves, and the evolution of surf wear and gear.

Perhaps best of all, you'll always find helpful docents on hand – lifelong surfers keen to share their knowledge and stories. Through their commitment to education and preservation, the sport is highlighted, along with its impact on lifestyle, art, and culture. So, whether you're a die-hard surfer or just a fan, a visit offers a fun, comprehensive look at a sport that's captivated millions around the globe.

Address 312 Pier View Way, Oceanside, CA 92054, +1 (760) 721-6876, www.surfmuseum.org, csm@surfmuseum.org | Getting there Bus 101, 302, 303, 313, 318, 392 or 395; Coaster to Oceanside Transit Center | Hours Daily 10am–4pm | Tip Visit the Imperial Beach Outdoor Surf Museum, a display of full-sized, tubular outlines of surfboards representing board designs over time (Palm Avenue and 3rd Street, Imperial Beach, www.imperialbeachca.gov).

15 Cancer… There's Hope

A park dedicated to survival

Sitting directly across the road from the San Diego International Airport, along the waterfront of Spanish Landing Park, is the Richard and Annette Bloch Cancer Survivors Park; a small park with a delicate water feature and pathways for passersby. At the heart of the park is the powerful sculpture *Cancer… There's Hope* by Mexican sculptor Victor Salmones. This bronze piece features three figures: a man, a woman, and a child, hand-in-hand, and clearly happy. This represents the group escaping the maze that is cancer, embodying the journey of survivorship and the strength required to overcome the disease. The people entering the maze behind them depict those who have been diagnosed with cancer and their loved ones, and the journey that they are about to embark on.

Salmones, celebrated for his evocative and expressive works in bronze, captured the essence of hope and resilience in this sculpture. Unfortunately, this was Salmones' last sculpture; he was diagnosed with cancer just two weeks after completing the work and passed away shortly after.

The park is a creation of the Richard and Annette Bloch Foundation, established by Richard Bloch, co-founder of H&R Block, and his wife Annette. After Richard's own battle with lung cancer in 1978, and his subsequent remission, the couple dedicated their lives to supporting others facing similar battles. The foundation's mission is to provide resources, fund research, and create helpful environments like the Cancer Survivors Parks.

San Diego's park is part of a broader network of Richard and Annette Bloch Cancer Survivors Parks located in various cities, including Kansas City, Houston, and Indianapolis. Each park shares the common goal of supporting cancer survivors and their families, and being a place where every step you take is a tribute to the journey of cancer survivorship and the unyielding spirit of those who fight.

Address Spanish Landing, 3572-3678 North Harbor Drive, San Diego, CA 92101 | Getting there Bus 923 to N Harbor Park Drive & Lee Court | Hours Unrestricted | Tip While at Spanish Landing Park, find California Historical Landmark No. 891, which marks the site of the Spanish Portolá expedition landing with Gaspar de Portolá and Father Junípero Serra on May 4–5, 1769 (just west of the Cancer Survivors Park).

16 Casa y Cocina

A passion for Mexican culture and craft

Right in the heart of North Park is one of creative entrepreneur Elexia de la Parra's newest ventures: Casa y Cocina. Embarking on this journey, de la Parra has introduced a curated boutique featuring home and tabletop items that embody the essence of Mexico.

De la Parra's original North Park gem is the beloved Artelexia, which is also a celebration of Mexican culture and traditions. With its vibrant displays and hand-sourced items, it's a love letter to Mexico's rich heritage and craftsmanship offering a unique blend of gifts, décor, and artisanal products.

The inspiration for Casa y Cocina stemmed from de la Parra's travels and buying trips for Artelexia, when she encountered a myriad of items that spoke to her heart. With this shop, she aspires to encapsulate the ambiance of quaint village shops, the charm of European-style general stores, and the bustling energy of Mexican *mercados*. At its core, Casa y Cocina brings Mexican artisans and Latinx-owned businesses into the spotlight. Its embrace, however, is global, celebrating unique works from around the world and transporting her shoppers to places well outside their own *casas* and *cocinas*.

Traditional designs, exceptional artistry, and an array of decorative items make this a must-visit shop for those seeking the best in home and kitchen adornments. Aside from gorgeous home goods, Casa y Cocina tempts the taste buds with a selection of Mexican small-batch delicacies and gourmet food treasures from both local makers and artisans across the border.

Visit the shop and stock up on an assortment of Talavera pottery, *michelada* supplies (the mix, the glasses, the garnishes!), and fiesta necessities, or have a custom goodie box made within your budget to add an element of surprise. Regardless of what you're in the mood for, there's something beautiful and delicious waiting for you at Casa y Cocina.

Address 3030 N Park Way, San Diego, CA 92104, +1 (619) 380-2447, www.casaycocina.com, customerservice@casaycocina.com | Getting there Bus 2, 6, 7 or 10 to University Avenue & 30th Street | Hours Mon–Sat 11am–6pm, Sun 11am–5pm | Tip While in the neighborhood, check out a show at The Observatory, a historic live music venue that's been around since 1929 (2891 University Avenue, www.observatorysd.com).

17 Chino Family Farm

From WWII internment camp to acclaimed farm

Resting comfortably in the middle of Rancho Santa Fe is a decades-old farm where green corn husks jut out of a valley situated just east of the Pacific, and mist from the marine layer sits atop the emerald leaves of vegetables to be sold at the roadside stand. It's the picture of perfection.

So it's no surprise that both local and not-so-local chefs consider Chino Farms to be their go-to spot for fresh produce. In fact, culinary powerhouses like Wolfgang Puck, Alice Waters, and Ruth Reichl have been known to seek out the locally grown specialty ingredients.

Considering the farm's loyal following and pristine produce, some may be shocked to know the difficult history of the family behind it, and the hardships they've endured to get to where they are today.

Junzo Chino, the original owner of the farm, immigrated to the US from a small Japanese fishing village in the early 1920s. He wed and had children, and over the years the family moved around, grew vegetable seedlings, flowers, and peppers. In 1942, the entire family was sent to a Japanese internment camp. Upon returning to California three and a half years later, the Chinos had nothing, and because of alien land laws, they couldn't purchase land and continue farming. In 1946, friends were able to secure some land for them to lease, and in 1952 Chino purchased 56 acres in the middle of Rancho Santa Fe. The Vegetable Shop opened as a roadside stand in the summer of '69 and is still run by the family to this day.

Known for the sweetest corn imaginable, Mara de Bois French strawberries, and a unique produce selection, the shop sells only fresh goods grown on site, using a combination of traditional Japanese farming techniques and modern innovations. The farm is also well-known in Japan, and Japanese trainees often come to work in the greenhouses and fields, and to study the Chinos' methods and guiding principles.

Address 6123 Calzada Del Bosque, Rancho Santa Fe, CA 92091, +1 (858) 756-3184 | Getting there Bus 308 to Via De La Valle & Calzada Del Bosque | Hours Wed–Sat 10am–3:30pm | Tip Head a little further into Rancho Santa Fe and indulge in drool-worthy baked goods at the picturesque Thyme in the Ranch (16905 Avenida de Acacias, Rancho Santa Fe, www.thymeintheranch.com).

18 Coin-Op Game Room

Where adults get their game on

At Coin-Op Game Room in North Park, you walk in and immediately feel it: the energy of a bar that knows how to have fun without taking itself too seriously. It's a combo of laughter, sounds from the arcade machines, and, if you're lucky, the smell of pretzel bites fresh out of the oven.

The games here are a perfect mix of old-school and crowd favorites. There's Ms. Pac-Man, Street Fighter, Galaga – the classics you can play by memory – and a few surprise pinball machines, like *The Mandalorian* and *Jurassic Park,* that draw everyone in for a quick game. Some people go all in, focused on beating their own high scores, while others just play for fun, seeing who can last the longest before that inevitable "Game Over" screen. There is also a handful of four-player games for those who want to get competitive with their crew.

When it comes to drinks, Coin-Op nails it. They offer a solid variety of craft beers on tap and a sweet selection of simple cocktails designed more for sipping than fussing over. You can tell they're made to pair with the vibe here – casual, flavorful, no unnecessary frills.

And the food? It's exactly what you want when you're mid-game. TJ hot dogs (bacon-wrapped, all-beef dogs with onion, bell pepper, jalapeños, and garlic aioli) with just the right kick, plus corn dog bites you can eat one-handed, perfect for bouncing between games and drinks. It's comfort food that doesn't slow you down – who has time to sit when there's a high score to beat?

Perhaps best of all, if you show up on the last Sunday of the month, Free Play Sunday is where it's at – no quarters required. You can settle in for hours, rotating from game to game and trying new ones just because you can. And if you're here during Happy Hour from Tuesday to Friday, the deals on drinks and snacks make it hard to leave, even if you only meant to pop in for one quick round.

Address 3926 30th Street, San Diego, CA 92104, +1 (619) 255-8523, www.coinopgameroom.com, info@coinopsd.com | Getting there Bus 2, 6, 7 or 10 to 30th Street & University Avenue | Hours Mon–Thu 5pm–midnight, Fri 5pm–2am, Sat 2pm–2am, Sun 2pm–midnight | Tip Try your hand at more games, like shuffleboard and bocce ball, or sing your heart out at karaoke, all while indulging in killer cocktails and grub at Punchbowl Social (1485 E Street, www.punchbowlsocial.com).

19 Collins & Coupe

Local shrubs and tiki mugs

On El Cajon Boulevard in San Diego's North Park neighborhood is where you'll find Collins & Coupe, a well-stocked cocktail shop that is as perfectly curated as it is Insta-worthy. Since Logan Mitchell and Gary McIntire opened the store back in 2017, this 1,000-square-foot boutique has emerged as a must-visit for cocktail lovers, seamlessly marrying the allure of vintage aesthetics with cutting-edge libation trends.

Notably, Collins & Coupe proudly showcases products from Black, POC, women, and LGBTQIA+-owned businesses, embodying a spirit of inclusivity and support for the local community, and creating a conscious celebration of culture and creativity that's mirrored in every item on the shelf, many of which are locally produced.

The vintage collection here is both a nod to the elegance of mixology and the campiness of some of the wares. You're not going to stumble upon any old thrift store finds here, but rather meticulously chosen glassware, classic ashtrays, whimsical tiki mugs, and sleek decanters. For those venturing into the world of cocktail crafting, the shop also offers a great range of bar essentials, including professional equipment, delectable syrups, shrubs, garnishes, and more.

Ice, an often-overlooked cocktail component, receives its due limelight here. The boutique features unique ice forms, from pristine clear to artistically tumbled, and some imported all the way from Japan to add a visual allure and elevated quality to the drinks. And for those not partaking in booze, the selection of mocktails, sodas, and other beverages ensures every sip is an indulgent one.

Products aside, Collins & Coupe's allure extends beyond its shopping experience. Their regular classes and other events bring together the community, both professionals and the home mixologists alike, ensuring its place as a mainstay in San Diego's cocktail culture.

Address 2876 El Cajon Boulevard, No. 100, San Diego, CA 92104, +1 (619) 727-4971, www.collinsandcoupe.com, collinsandcoupe@gmail.com | Getting there Bus 1 or 6 to El Cajon Boulevard & Utah Street | Hours Mon–Thu 11am–7pm, Fri–Sun 10am–7pm | Tip Check out the 90-foot-long mural, dinosaur décor, and impressive selection of vintage books at nearby Verbatim Books (3793 30th Street, www.verbatimbooks.com).

20 The Comedy Store

Bringing the laughs since '76

There are few things in life that are better than a good laugh, and the Comedy Store in La Jolla is there to make sure life is full of 'em. It opened back in 1976, three years after the original club opened on Sunset Boulevard in Los Angeles, where the owner, Mitzi Shore, opened a room in Pacific Beach so comedians could perform and test out new material in a smaller, more intimate space. In 1977, the perfect, permanent place became available at an old disco in La Jolla, and Shore leased it right away.

With Shore's connections, the new location was able to attract some of the best performers out there, including Richard Pryor and Robin Williams, and have them work their magic on a regular basis. In fact, David Letterman was there to tell the first joke on opening night. For the comedians, it was a testing ground for new material and a space to unwind away from the intensity of the Hollywood scene. For San Diegans, it was a way to get a comedy fix without having to make the trip to LA. And if you want to hone your own skills, sign up for a six-week stand-up comedy workshop for aspiring comedians at all levels.

Today, the Comedy Store is booked solid with some of the funniest humans on Earth. On weekends, the pros from LA come out, and during the week, local (albeit still pro) comedians perform. On Tuesdays, the Comedy Store has an open-mic night where anyone can try their hand at being hilarious, and there's no cover. On the last Wednesday of every month, they host "Pretty Funny Women," an all-female stand-up show that was created by comedian Lisa Sundstedt back in 1995. To this day, it is the longest-running all-female stand-up show in the world.

Of course, the best part of the Comedy Store is that it's a guaranteed good time. It doesn't hurt that tickets are usually inexpensive, it's in a central location, and they have the best popcorn in town.

Address 916 Pearl Street, La Jolla, CA 92037, +1 (858) 454-9176, www.thecomedystore.com/la-jolla, lajolla@comedystore.com | Getting there Bus 30 to Pearl Street & Fay Avenue or Girard Avenue & Torrey Pines Road | Hours See website for showtimes; ages 21+ only, ID required | Tip For more stand-up comedy, podcast recordings, and themed comedy events, check out Clairmont's Mic Drop Comedy (8878 Clairemont Mesa Boulevard, www.micdropcomedy.com).

21 Convoy Music Bar

A hidden spot for the discerning audiophile

Listening bars are popular in Japan, especially in Tokyo's Shibuya district. They're outfitted with exceptional sound systems and serve up creative cocktails and sometimes small bites, but the focus is on experiencing the music itself. Modeled after these unique spots, Convoy Music Bar provides that kind of experience, and then some.

To find this secret spot, visitors must head to the strip mall at 4646 Convoy Street, which houses The Taco Stand, O'Brien's Pub, and a handful of other beloved eateries. Next, go to the right of O'Brien's toward the back of the strip mall and turn left into the small alleyway. It's long, narrow, and a legit functioning alley, garbage dumpsters and all. But just behind The Taco Stand, a red "On Air" sign above a nondescript door means you've arrived.

Guests are greeted with an *oshibori*, a hot or cold (depending on the season) moist hand towel to cleanse their hands upon arrival, and are guided into a small, 40-seat space that oozes style and elegance. Velvet-lined surfaces, brass touches, and a backlit bar give speakeasy vibes, while the extensive vinyl collection and low, intimate seating areas create a cozy, relaxing atmosphere.

The menu is small and mainly consists of spirit-forward cocktails, many playing on popular drinks like the Jungle Bird and Old Fashioned. There is also an impressive Japanese whiskey selection and a handful of other options (like wine and Japanese beer) for those looking for something other than the hard stuff.

Each night, a soundtrack for the evening is created and played by a guest DJ, with songs from the eclectic vinyl selection filling the space via a custom set of Kenrick speakers imported from Japan.

To keep the experience pure and music-focused, there is a strict dress code, and no flash-photography is allowed, ensuring patrons get an authentic taste of a Tokyo-style listening bar. (And yes, even the bathrooms are equipped with Japanese high-tech toilets.)

Address 4646 Convoy Street, No. 112, San Diego, CA 92111, +1 (858) 251-6340, www.convoymusicbar.com, hello@convoymusicbar.com | Getting there Bus 27 to Balboa Avenue & Convoy Street, or bus 44 to Convoy & Dagget Streets | Hours Sun, Mon, Wed, Thu 5pm–midnight, Fri & Sat 5pm–1am | Tip Fill your belly before imbibing with handmade *xiao long bao* (steamed dumplings) across the street at the Dumpling Inn & Shanghai Saloon (4625 Convoy Street, www.dumplinginn.com).

22 Coronado Ferry

Take the scenic route

Operating in the sparkling waters of the bay, the Coronado Ferry has been a crucial link between San Diego and Coronado Island since 1886. The story of the ferry begins in the late 19th century, when the then-remote island was only accessible by boat. The ferry's value surged with the opening of the Hotel del Coronado in 1888, and it remained the primary link between San Diego and Coronado Island for decades.

Today, the 15-minute ferry ride is a quick but beautiful adventure. As the ferry makes its way across the bay, you can enjoy gorgeous views of the San Diego skyline, the San Diego–Coronado Bridge, and the USS *Midway* Museum. You may even catch occasional glimpses of playful dolphins or sea lions. The trip is especially good for those looking to take unique photos of the city.

Flagship Cruises, a local and family-owned company, runs the two ferries for the route: the *Silvergate* and the *Cabrillo*. The 65-foot-long *Silvergate* was built in 1940 and is the longest-running wooden ferry in the country, so when you embark on it, you're riding aboard a piece of maritime history. Though the bridge offers a faster route, the ferry is the perfect choice for a leisurely journey. It's also affordable at just $9 each way, and kids under the age of four ride for free.

It's important to note that these ferries are for passengers only, and vehicles must cross the bay via the bridge. But the ferry boats do allow passengers to take their bicycles on board without an additional charge, and there are rental bikes available upon arrival at the Coronado Ferry Landing. Coronado Island is the perfect place to explore on two wheels.

Once you're across the bay, explore the charming streets, enjoy the beaches, or simply savor the sea breeze. Sure, the ferry is a great way to get from point A to B, but it's so much more. Next time, take the scenic route.

Address Broadway Pier, 990 North Harbor Drive, San Diego, CA 92101, +1 (619) 234-4111, www.flagshipsd.com | Getting there Surfliner to Santa Fe Depot; bus 923 or 992 to North Harbor Drive & Broadway | Hours See website for daily schedule | Tip Head across the street from the Broadway Pier to Lane Field, the former home of the San Diego Padres (1009 North Harbor Drive).

23 Datura

Witchy wares and whatnots

This quaint boutique on 30th Street is a haven for those drawn to the mystical and eclectic. Named after the enchanting plant known in folklore as a "witches' weed," Datura is a portal into a world where magic and the modern mingle. Owned by Kristy Nadine, a talented tattoo artist and co-owner of Crybaby Tattoo, the shop reflects her artistic journey, which began with her Earth and Bone jewelry line, and has now blossomed into this unique store.

Visitors are greeted by a bright ambiance filled with natural light, showing off the store's beautifully arranged array of products. Datura's shelves are lined with an impressive selection of ethically and sustainably sourced herbs, roots, and dried mushrooms. The shop's dedication to sustainability extends to its collection of bones and feathers, all ethically sourced, ensuring that each item has a story that respects both nature and craft.

Each corner of Datura is filled with oddities and curios, ranging from natural, uncut crystals to meticulously crafted, handmade jewelry. For those seeking to enhance their spiritual practice, Datura offers an array of candles designed for witchcraft, spell work, or simply indulgence. Inside the shop, the scent of incense and ritual resins permeates the air, alongside bundles of sage smudges for cleansing rituals.

For the divination enthusiast, Datura doesn't disappoint. The store boasts a diverse collection of tarot, astrological, and fortune-telling cards, alongside a variety of altar items. Adding to the allure is a full line of bath and body products, allowing customers to carry a bit of Datura's magic into their daily lives.

Nadine's move from Colorado to San Diego in 2013 has culminated in the creation of this magical space. An ode to her passion for the artistic and the esoteric, it's a small sanctuary for those who find beauty in the unconventional and the magical.

Address 3552 30th Street, San Diego, CA 92104, www.earthandbone.com | **Getting there** Bus 2 to 30th & Dwight Streets, or bus 7 or 10 to University Avenue & 30th Street | **Hours** Wed–Sun noon–6pm | **Tip** Looking for more gemstones? Head over to the nearby Cave of Wonders for a wide assortment of minerals and gems (3819 Ray Street, www.thecaveofwonders.com).

24 Dave's Rock Garden

The community garden that keeps on growing

Back in 2015, Dave Dean decided to clean up one of the lots near Moonlight Beach. The lot, one of many state-owned pieces of property nearby, was overrun with weeds and drug paraphernalia. Not only did he clean it up, but he also started planting.

He was eventually served with a cease-and-desist order, but as nothing came of it, Dean kept on planting at night, when nobody from the state could tell him not to. Luckily, there was a big hedge that hid his progress. When the garden, complete with pathways and an American flag, was done, he took down the hedge. He ended up getting support from the state, and the space has become a special spot for anyone who comes across it.

Now, about the rocks. When Dean was building the pathways in the garden, he opted to line them with stones. Each day, he would go to the beach and pick up a few stones and take them back to the garden. One day, someone dropped off a painted rock and put it right at the beginning of one of his pathways. He liked the idea, so he and a few friends opted to do the same – pick up rocks at the beach and paint them. Over time, people started bringing their own painted rocks to add, and a few local artists even contribute(d) regularly.

Today, Dean has placed over 8,000 rocks painted by people from at least 120 different countries. "It's really developed into being part of the fabric of the community," says Dean, "It's a safe space."

Visitors are invited to come to the garden with their own rocks. Dean is usually there between 8am and noon on Saturdays and Sundays, and he provides paint and brushes. After the paint dries, he brushes each rock with a few coats of varnish before displaying them.

Whether or not you paint a rock for the garden, there's plenty to look at. Little tree-stump stools are placed throughout the space, so people have a place to sit, meditate, read, or just relax.

Address 200-298 B Street, Encinitas, CA 92024, www.davesrockgarden.com | Getting there Coaster to Encinitas; bus 101 to Encinitas Boulevard & Vulcan Avenue | Hours Unrestricted | Tip On Sundays, head to the Leucadia Farmers Market at Paul Ecke Central Elementary and check out their School Garden (185 Union Street, Encinitas, www.instagram.com/pec_garden).

25 Diversionary Theatre

Entertainment, empowerment, and representation

Born out of a need for a space that could give a voice to the widely marginalized LGBTQIA+ community affected by the HIV/AIDS epidemic in the mid-1980s, University Heights-based Diversionary Theatre has addressed that need, and so much more, for nearly 40 years. In fact, it is the third-oldest continually operating LGBTQIA+ theater of its kind in the country. It has not only helped share the stories of a diverse group of people, but it has also aimed to empower individuals of all ages and walks of life.

Through live entertainment and a variety of other programs, Diversionary has created an inclusive place for those looking to share stories and amplify the presence of the diverse queer community in San Diego. The organization emphasizes the importance of uplifting all groups in need of social justice and positive change, including those who are Black, Indigenous, and people of color (BIPOC).

On the main floor, the Austin & Joann Clark Cabaret has become a safe, liberating space for local LGBTQIA+ people seeking nightlife, community, and accessible arts programs. The cabaret is open five nights per week, providing mostly free, live, LGBTQIA+-centered entertainment such as music, storytelling, film screenings, comedy, and other arts events in a casual, stylish patio and piano bar atmosphere. It also features a permanent historical display created in partnership with the Lambda Archives of San Diego commemorating the space in the tradition of the iconic "Gay Bar," where the LGBTQIA+ community and movement united.

In the main theaters, both original and internationally known musicals, performances by up-and-coming artists, and queer-themed entertainment thrive. Meanwhile, the Diversionary arts department offers free programs year-round. Summer camps, annual festivals, and so much more are also available for people of all ages and orientations.

Address 4545 Park Boulevard, No. 101, San Diego, CA 92116, +1 (619) 220-0097, www.diversionary.org, boxoffice@diversionary.org | Getting there Bus 11 to Park Boulevard & Monroe Avenue (parking nearby is extremely limited) | Hours Box office Tue–Sat noon–6pm, Clark Cabaret & Bar Wed–Mon 5pm–close, Sun 1–7pm | Tip Grab a pizza and a pint at Hillcrest Brewing Company, the first openly gay brewery in the world (1458 University Avenue, www.hillcrestbrewingcompany.com).

26 The Dog Society

Where pups take their people

Tucked away in San Diego's Rolando neighborhood, The Dog Society is simply the perfect place for dog lovers and their furry friends. This spot redefines the concept of pet-friendly places, mixing canine care with good old fun in a versatile, fun space.

Extending over 8,500 square feet, The Dog Society venue was once a furniture store but has been transformed into a social hub for people and pups! For the dogs, there are both indoor and outdoor play areas where they can frolic freely and engage in social play in a secure, supervised environment. The play areas are designed to cater to all kinds of dogs, ensuring safety and fun for every breed and personality.

While the pooches enjoy their playtime, their human companions are not left behind. The Dog Society has a café and bar, where owners can unwind and socialize with a tasty menu offering: everything from light snacks, like açaí bowls and paninis, to pub favorites, like nachos and chicken wings. The beverage selection is equally varied, with coffee shop mainstays, wine, beer, cocktails, and kombucha on tap.

Of course, there's fun for the people, too. The space features a full-sized shuffleboard court, cornhole, pool table, and televisions so you catch a game from the perfect spot. The outdoor beer garden offers guests the best of both worlds, where you can sip on a drink in the sunshine while your pups can hang out off-leash in the space. Don't worry, you're not the only one who can sip on a wee pint. The folks at The Dog Society also offer a trio of "dog beer" (pork, beef, or veggie), and a handful of special, pooch-friendly snacks.

In addition to their usual offerings, The Dog Society also hosts regular meetups for different breeds (think Frenchie Friday or Poodles and Doodles!) in the hopes of fostering a sense of community among dog lovers, and events, like a neon cornhole party, to keep things fun.

Address 6331 University Avenue, San Diego, CA 92115, +1 (619) 780-0235, www.dogsocietysd.com | Getting there Bus 852 to University Avenue & Rolando Boulevard or University Avenue & Bonillo Drive | Hours Mon, Thu & Fri 4–10pm, Wed 4–9pm, Sat 11am–10pm, Sun 10am–8pm | Tip Treat your pup or feline friend to some homemade treats and specialty goods at Dexter's Deli (locations in San Diego, Carlsbad, and Del Mar, www.dextersdeli.com).

27 Downstairs at David Alan

Channel your inner explorer

Located on Cedros Avenue in Solana Beach's Design District, the David Alan Collection is celebrated for its custom wood furniture and globally sourced artifacts, particularly its stunning heirloom-quality, wood slab tables crafted from reclaimed timber. Each piece is made with precision craftsmanship, and the beauty and integrity of the grain comes through. You can even find some of their gorgeous tables in local spots like Carruth Cellars just down the street. But if you really want to unearth the magic of this gallery, head down to the basement.

Affectionately dubbed the "Indiana Jones Warehouse," this 8,000-square-foot space is an adventurer's dream. While it doesn't boast any stolen relics or mythical treasures, it does offer up an unparalleled collection of rare artifacts from Southeast Asia and beyond. The basement is divided into two areas: part workshop, where the oh-so-talented woodworkers fabricate and refinish pieces like said signature slab tables; and part treasure trove, featuring one-of-a-kind items curated from remote villages across Asia.

This collection includes original tribal art, much of it centuries old, alongside folk art, petrified wood, ancient stone carvings, copper cauldrons, and spirit houses. You'll discover pieces from Indonesia, Thailand, Laos, Japan, China, and Nepal, each hand-selected for its authenticity and cultural significance. The mix of items and history creates a space that makes you feel like you're tiptoeing in some sort of back room of a museum. You feel like you shouldn't be there, but every item you see is meant to be admired. And best of all, it's all for sale!

Whether you're drawn to the primitive relief carvings or intricate sculptures, no two visits are ever the same. The inventory is constantly refreshed, so even seasoned treasure hunters will find something new and exciting with every trip.

Address 241 Cedros Avenue, Solana Beach, San Diego, CA 92075, +1 (858) 481-8044, www.thedavidalancollection.com, davidalancollection@gmail.com | Getting there Bus 101 or 308 to Highway 101 & Plaza Street | Hours Mon–Sat 9:30am–5:30pm, Sun 10am–5pm | Tip Head next door to SoLo, a unique collective curated by eight creative women (309 South Cedros Avenue, www.solocedros.com).

28 Eagle Mining Co.

A look at life underground

As you're making your way towards this mine, it might seem a little strange. After all, the mine is tucked right into the town of Julian, at the end of C Street, literally walking distance to shops, restaurants, and the best apple pie you could ever ask for. That said, once you've walked down that dirt road, there's no mistaking it: you've arrived at Eagle Mining Co.

Dug out by hand in the late 1800s, the mine's tunnels stretch deep into the hillside on a property dotted with old machinery and buildings. You'll feel transported to a completely different era that includes panning for gold, wearing candles on your head, and yelling "Eureka!" on a (hopefully) regular basis.

The tours at Eagle Mine are fascinating and roughly an hour long. The guide takes you through the cool, narrow passages, giving you a history lesson with a bit of geology thrown in along the way. You get a sense of the conditions the miners worked in, the cramped spaces, and the reliance on rudimentary equipment. It's a straightforward look at the past with no theatrics, just the real story. As you reach the end of the tunnels, keep an eye out for the bat that's made itself at home on the cave wall!

One of the unique aspects of the Eagle Mine is that it connects to the High Peak Mine, a neighboring operation. The two mines worked independently for years. They eventually linked up so they could share resources and equipment, which made operations more efficient in the rough mining days.

After you've explored the tunnels, it's time to try a bit of gold panning. Nothing touristy, just a quick chance to get your hands wet in the same pursuit that brought so many people to these hills back in the day. The property also has a small collection of antiques and a museum that offers an interesting mix of mining artifacts and local curiosities. It's well worth a few extra minutes to wander through.

Address 2320 C Street, Julian, CA 92036, +1 (760) 765-0036, www.theeaglemining.com, eaglemine2019@gmail.com | Getting there By car, from Main Street in Julian, head northeast on C Street. Turn right at the end of the road. | Hours Daily 10am–5pm | Tip Sure, Julian is famous for its apple pie, but head on over to the Julian Pie Company and give their apple crumble a shot (2225 Main Street, www.julianpie.com).

29 El Campo Santo Cemetery

Laid to rest, and buried twice

Right in the middle of Old Town, El Campo Santo Cemetery is a silent storyteller of the city's past. It was first established in 1849 as a Roman Catholic cemetery. It served as the sacred resting place for early European settlers, Native Americans, and an assortment of well-known characters, like "Yankee Jim" Robinson, a notorious criminal from California's rough beginnings. Between its founding and 1880, 477 bodies were buried there. In 1889, a line for horse-drawn streetcars was built through part of the cemetery, which later became San Diego Avenue.

Restoration efforts in the 1930s revitalized the cemetery in hopes of preserving its tales for future generations, and the adobe wall that surrounds the cemetery was built in 1933. Less than 10 years later, the streetcar line was paved over, leaving many graves under the road. In fact, one of the headstones within the cemetery states, "Bill Marshall is not here. But on the other side of the wall."

Fast-forward 50 years, when ground-penetrating radar was used to locate buried bodies under San Diego Avenue. Today, small round metal discs marked "Grave Site" indicate the various locations of the concealed graves, offering a small reminder of those who lie beneath.

Naturally, plenty of rumors of spiritual activity swirl around El Campo Santo. People have claimed to see apparitions and feel bursts of cold, and some have even complained of their cars not starting when parked on the paved-over portion of the cemetery. These stories have drawn thrill-seekers and ghost hunters to the area for years.

On a more historical and culturally significant note, El Campo Santo is, of course, an important part of Old Town during the pre-Hispanic tradition of *Día de Los Muertos*. The cemetery and surrounding area are decorated with stunning *ofrendas*, or offerings, and it's where the elaborate, candlelit procession ends.

Address 2410 San Diego Avenue, San Diego, CA 92110, www.oldtownsandiego.org/el-campo-santo-second-oldest-cemetery-in-san-diego | Getting there Bus 8, 9, 10, 28, 30, 35, 44, 83,84, 88, or 105; Coaster or Pacific Surfliner to Old Town Transit Center | Hours Unrestricted | Tip Take a stroll along the nearby Heritage Park Row to see some historic homes, like the Bushyhead House and Christian House (Old Town, www.oldtownsandiego.org).

30 Encinitas Boat Houses

Landlocked nautical treasures

Sitting smack between the beach and the bustling 101 are the whimsical boat houses SS *Encinitas* and SS *Moonlight*. No, not houseboats, but boat houses. Built in the 1920s by the visionary Miles Minor Kellogg (no relation to the father of the cereal industry), these architectural marvels resembling ships ready to set sail are anchored firmly on 3rd Street.

Crafted from salvaged materials of the once-lively Moonlight Beach Dance Pavilion and Bathhouse, the boat houses are an architectural treat and a great showcase for Kellogg's recycling skills as an early adopter. They reflect the city's commitment to innovation and sustainability, a concept Kellogg pioneered long before it became a global movement. Even today, as we grapple with environmental concerns, these houses serve as a good reminder of the potential of upcycling and sustainable living.

The boat houses, nearly identical, were made to not only look like real boats, but they are also to scale, and they had masts, bowsprits, and anchors until the mid-20th century. The maritime magic of these structures, with their curved roofs and nautical-themed windows (including faux hatches that are actually skylights, and wooden shelves built to look like stairs leading up to the skylights), create an illusion of ocean-going vessels, albeit forever anchored on land. They're a quirky juxtaposition against the backdrop of the typical Californian landscape and the more traditional-looking homes that surround them.

While the boats remain private residences and are not open for tours, the sight of them is enough to make visitors see that creativity knows no bounds, and that history always intertwines with the present. In fact, apparently there's no documented credible explanation for why Kellogg chose to build the homes in such a fantastical way, but his imagination is still appreciated a century later.

Address 726–732 3rd Street, Encinitas, CA 92024, www.encinitashistoricalsociety.org/the-boathouses, info@encinitashistoricalsociety.org | Getting there Bus 101 to Highway 101 & H Street; Coaster to Encinitas | Hours Viewable from the outside only | Tip History buffs, make your way over to F Street and check out the 1883 Schoolhouse, which also houses the Encinitas Historical Society (390 West F Street, Encinitas).

31 Encinitas House of Art

Get creative at open studio nights

Located in downtown Encinitas, the Encinitas House of Art is a creative space for anyone looking to explore art in a welcoming and relaxed environment. Its Open Studio Nights, however, are where it's at. They're designed for all ages and skill levels and provide a fun, easy, approachable way to dive into art without any pressure. Just show up with an open mind and a can-do attitude, and you're good to go.

All supplies are included: paints, canvases, brushes, sculpting tools, glitter (so much glitter), paper, you name it – so there's no need to bring anything. The space itself is charming, with nearly every surface covered in paint, glue, and sparkles, setting the stage for a laid-back creative experience. While the sessions are self-guided, the studio's in-house artists are available to offer advice and tips to help bring your ideas to life.

The Open Studio setup is casual and flexible, so it's perfect for any occasion, be it a date night, team-building event, evenings with friends, or even just some solo time to unwind and try something new. You're encouraged to bring your own food and drinks to enjoy while creating, but make sure it's something easy to eat like a slice of pizza from the nearby Gelati & Peccati, washed down with a freshly poured crowler from Culture Brewing across the street, or a well-stocked charcuterie board. Just remember to dress for the weather, since the studio is essentially an indoor/outdoor space.

Attending an Open Studio Night isn't about making a masterpiece, though if you're there to get your Michelangelo on, go you! It's about stepping out of your routine and comfort zone, embracing creativity, and enjoying the process. Whatever your skill level may be, a seasoned artist or a first-timer with a paint brush, the House of Art provides the tools, space, and atmosphere to make something that is uniquely yours.

Address 812 2nd Street, Encinitas, CA 92024, www.encinitashouseofart.com, info@encinitashouseofart.com | Getting there Bus 101 to Highway 101 & H Street; Coaster to Encinitas | Hours See website for events schedule; reservation required | Tip While you're in a creative groove, head north to the Mudd House and learn how to use a pottery wheel, make handcrafted clay items, or check out their BYOB Happy Hour that includes a quick demo (802 N Coast Highway 101, Encinitas, www.themuddhousestudio.com).

32 The Euclid Tower

An 80-foot-tall blast from the past

If you've ever driven down University Avenue in City Heights, you've probably seen the Euclid Tower. While it's certainly a defined part of the area's skyline, it's an odd one. Built in 1932, the tower began as a perfect example of Art Deco style, though, believe it or not, the architect is unknown. Originally designed as part of a theater, it was to be a unique drive-in soda fountain where customers could pull up, grab a drink at the ground-floor counter, and head up to a glass-walled observation deck to check out the view over the growing neighborhood. This style of drive-in dining was unusual for its time and quickly made the tower a favorite local spot.

As years passed, the tower hosted a mix of businesses, adapting with the times. In the 1940s and '50s, it shifted to other uses, becoming home to small local eateries and later to beauty shops. By then, the soda fountain era had faded, and while the Euclid Tower's Art Deco lines were still eye-catching amid the changing storefronts in the neighborhood, the colors had faded, and it turned into more of a gray, sad-looking structure.

In 1995, a community art project transformed part of the tower with vibrant ceramic tiles made by local third-grade students. Each tile illustrated scenes from City Heights life. This addition marked a new chapter for the tower by linking it to the neighborhood's identity and adding a distinctly local touch. That's not the end of the story, however.

In 1999, safety concerns led to the removal of the tower's spire, which had long defined its silhouette. It stood without its iconic peak until 2009, when a restoration project brought a new, slightly shorter spire, bringing back the structure's visual impact and keeping its classic look intact. Since then, the Euclid Tower has housed The Tower Bar, a laid-back, well-loved bar with a bit of a divey vibe, and an upstairs tattoo parlor.

Address 4757 University Avenue, San Diego, CA 92105 | Getting there Bus 7, 10 or 965 to University Avenue & 47th Street | Hours Unrestricted | Tip Take a look across the street at the building that houses Big City Liquor. Otherwise known as the Egyptian Garage, it's an incredible example of Egyptian Revival architecture, and was built in the beginning of the 1920s (4749 University Avenue).

33 Fallbrook Winery

Trading avocados for grapes

Fallbrook Winery is one of the oldest wineries in San Diego County, located in a high-elevation (for Southern California) area that's perfect for growing grapes. Some of the vines on the property are over 25 years old, giving their wines a certain *je ne sais quoi* that comes with such maturity.

The tasting room building, built into the hillside around 35 years ago, has underground caves that naturally stay cool year-round, making them ideal for storing and aging wine. The space itself is low-key, with a focus on function over flash. It's dark and cozy, in a historical-romance-novel kind of way, but the art from local artists, typically expressionist pieces, keeps the room grounded in this century.

In addition to its vines, the property is home to about 30 avocado trees that have been around for close to a century. While Fallbrook is typically known for its avocado production, the winery proves that there's plenty of reason to associate the area with wine, too. They make more than 20 wines on-site, offering a nice variety for visitors to try and plenty of bottles to bring home.

Winemaker Euan Parker brings over two decades of experience to his role at Fallbrook Winery. He began his career in New Zealand, working in his family's vineyards. After earning an honors degree in biochemistry, he received a full scholarship to the École Supérieure des Agricultures in Angers, France, where he completed a master's degree in Vine, Wine, and *Terroir* Management. Parker's international experience includes winemaking in Spain, France, and the US. Since joining Fallbrook, he has overseen all aspects of wine production, and he has built a lineup of wines that highlight the unique growing conditions of the region.

So while it may not be as glitzy as nearby wineries in Temecula, Fallbrook Winery delivers great wines in a relaxed, welcoming space that's well worth checking out.

Address 2554 Via Rancheros, Fallbrook, CA 92028, +1 (760) 0156, tastingroom@fallbrookwinery.com | Getting there By car from Main Avenue in downtown Fallbrook, head west toward South Mission Road, then go south, turn left on Winter Haven Road, continue onto Winterwarm Drive, and then take Via Rancheros to the winery | Hours Mon–Wed 10am–4:30pm, Thu–Sun 10am–6pm | Tip Take your pup (and maybe your human pals too) on an avocado farm adventure and picnic at the Choice Avocados farm (3450 West Sandia Creek Terrace, Fallbrook, www.choiceavocados.com).

34 *Fallen Star*

There's no place like home

Looking like it was precariously plunked atop the seventh floor of Jacobs Hall at the University of California San Diego, *Fallen Star* by South Korean artist Do Ho Suh is a mesmerizing combo of architecture and art that is indeed a quirky visual. But, even more, it is a thought-provoking look at displacement, home, and identity.

As you approach the building, your gaze is drawn upward by the sight of a quaint, blue house seemingly dropped from the sky and left hanging at a daring angle. It looks unsteady, but don't worry – it's been built to withstand 100-mile-per-hour winds and meets the state's earthquake code.

While it is quite the sight, the real magic is in and around the house itself. Its meticulously detailed exterior, from the manicured garden to the shingles and windows, invites you in to uncover the story behind this architectural anomaly.

Stepping into *Fallen Star* feels like entering another world. The interior is a perfect replica of a cozy, lived-in home, filled with books, photos, knick-knacks, and furniture. Yet the slight tilt of the house throws off your equilibrium upon entering, creating a disorienting physical experience that mirrors the emotional turbulence of being uprooted from one's home. This disorientation is no accident. Suh, drawing from his own experiences as an immigrant, designed the house to evoke the challenges and uncertainties of adapting to new surroundings. The tilted floor and skewed perspective are powerful metaphors for the instability and dislocation felt by those who find themselves in unfamiliar territory, and the physical feeling that accompanies the experience drives the analogy home.

While the building is not public, guided tours of the house are available, and the docents who host them are excellent storytellers, sharing the importance of *Fallen Star*'s profound statement on the nature of home and identity.

Address Jacobs Hall, Engineers Lane, San Diego, CA 92161, +1 (858) 534-2117, https://stuartcollection.ucsd.edu, stuartcollection@ucsd.edu | Getting there Bus 30, 41, 201 or 921 to Gilman Drive & Mandeville Lane, or bus 30, 101, 202, 479 or 974 to Gilman & Meyers Drives | Hours Scheduled tours only; reservation required | Tip While on campus, check out the Graffiti Art Park, a constantly changing outdoor art gallery (by the Student Center in the eucalyptus grove, to the east of the Stage Room).

35 Fishermen's Market of North County

Bringing the surf to the turf

Every Sunday morning, part of Oceanside Harbor turns into the Fishermen's Market of North County, where local fishermen offload their catch from the docks and practically into the hands of anyone looking for the freshest seafood around. Located just north of Joe's Crab Shack (there's extra parking near the beach, if you need it), the market offers local rockfish, halibut, mackerel, crabs, sardines, even sea urchins. It's not fancy – it's all about the fish, and that's the best part.

For the most part, the people running the stalls are the actual fishermen who go out on the boats, dealing with the grind of early mornings and rough waters. They're direct, approachable, and happy to explain what's fresh that day and suggest the best way to cook 'em. You'll hear conversations about the best frying techniques or someone sharing how to handle *uni* for the first time.

If you're used to grocery store seafood, the market might feel like a bit of a wake-up call. You're not going to find prepared fillets on Styrofoam trays or farmed fish from oceans away. The fish at the market isn't perfectly trimmed, and you might even have to clean it yourself, but that's part of the point. It's fresh, it's local, and it's as close as you'll get to catching it yourself without stepping onto a boat. For anyone who cares about the quality of what they eat or just wants a taste of Oceanside's fishing culture, this market is hard to beat.

Keep in mind that the market technically closes at two in the afternoon, but once they sell out, they shut down. So go early! The people who run the market are also working on bringing in more vendors selling coffee, pastries, and local produce to offer all of the ingredients for a complete, beautiful meal, and to round out your market experience.

Address 320 Harbor Drive, Oceanside, CA 92054, +1 (858) 633-3094, www.fishermensmarket.co | Getting there By car, take I-5 N to Harbor Drive. The market is located just north of Joe's Crab Shack. | Hours Sun 8am–2pm, or until sold out | Tip Not available on Sundays? Head to the nearby Harbor Pelican Market for a great selection of local fish, open daily from 7am to 5pm. They also serve up an assortment of prepared dishes like poke, ceviche, and grilled fish plates (1380 North Pacific Street, www.harborpelican.com).

36 Folk Arts Rare Records

Where the past and the present of music meet

Folk Arts Rare Records isn't just one of California's oldest record stores; it's proof of the city's rich musical heritage. This legendary shop, founded by Lou Curtiss, a key figure in the local music scene and the initiator of San Diego's first Folk Festival in 1967, goes beyond being a simple music store; it could even be called a landmark, mirroring the city's eclectic musical roots.

Curtiss' passion for music transformed the store into a place where people came to explore and discover new music (or, at least new to them) or dig up old favorites. When Brendan Boyle took over in 2014 and moved the shop to its current location on University Avenue, he inherited more than the store, but the legacy that Curtiss left him. Boyle's commitment to preserving the spirit of Folk Arts is evident in every corner of the space, with vintage posters and memorabilia making you feel like you've stepped back in time.

Naturally, the store is a haven for audiophiles. Its shelves are stocked with a wide range of LPs, 45s, 78s, CDs, and even 8-tracks, covering a variety of genres; you can find everything from folk music (obvi ously) to psychedelic, and everything in between.

This shop isn't just about the records, though, it's about the experience. The spacious layout, including a nice little listening area, invites leisurely, no-pressure browsing. While the friendly, knowledgeable staff are always on hand, ready to help you navigate through the vast, well-priced collection, you never feel like you're rushed into buying anything.

Its partnership with North Park's Part Time Lover Hi-Fi, which started back in 2022, has added a new dimension to Folk Arts. This collaboration brings the store's vibe beyond its regular retail space, expanding the community for fellow music lovers, and blending record shopping with a relaxed nightlife ambiance (and killer cocktails, to boot).

Address 3610 University Avenue, San Diego, CA 92104, +1 (619) 282-7833, www.folkartsrarerecords.com | Getting there Bus 7 to University & 36th Street | Hours Daily 10am–6pm | Tip Browse the South Park fave Vinyl Junkies for a unique, highly curated vinyl shopping experience (2235 Fern Street, www.vinyljunkies.net).

37__Fred's Urban Farm

Bringing greens to the people

Fred's Urban Farm in Spring Valley is a deliciously hidden gem on a quiet residential street, serving up a surprising and delightful variety of fresh, organic produce. This small-scale urban farm uses organic methods to grow a variety of nutrient-packed greens, and they specialize in microgreens, which are somewhere between a sprout and a baby green, and salad greens.

Founded during the pandemic, Fred's Urban Farm is run by Robin Kanzius, a former science teacher, and her son Kellen. Their vision began to come alive after they visited a microgreens operation at a market in Washington State, prompting them to start out with just 10 trays of microgreens in a closet. After realizing the potential that was right in front of them, including their perfect-for-permaculture property in East County, the farm grew.

The farm operates a self-service produce stand, where customers can find a range of seasonal goods, citrus, eggs, and, of course, microgreens. They also have other items, like their Electric Lemon Dressing. Payments are made on an honor system, with options for cash in a cash box, along with Venmo, and other methods via QR code. But it's not all about the farm stand itself. In addition to the Salad ATM, as locals affectionately call it, Fred's microgreens are also sold at a variety of grocery stores throughout the county, bringing the goodness to the broader community. Aside from fresh produce, Fred's Urban Farm also keeps bees, selling raw honey and even offering beekeeping classes! For those interested in growing their own microgreens, they provide grow kits and have online classes to help people cultivate these nutritional superstars at home.

The perfect example of an extraordinary place hiding in plain sight, Fred's Urban Farm offers nourishment, education, and a unique way of bringing sustainable agriculture and delicious foods to the San Diego community.

Address 3246 South Barcelona Street, Spring Valley, CA 91977, +1 (619) 559-6509, www.fredsurbanfarm.com, fredsurbanfarm@gmail.com | Getting there Bus 855 to Campo Road & Bonita Street, walk across Campo Road and down S Barcelona Street to the farm | Hours Daily 7am – 9pm | Tip Head to City Farmers Nursery and check out their beautiful selection of plants, learn how to start your own vegetable garden, or just hang out with the farm animals (3110 Euclid Avenue, www.cityfarmersnursery.com).

38 Free Fishing

Shelter Island's tiny pier is the perfect catch

To be clear, Shelter Island isn't really an island. While it feels like an island, it's actually a man-made peninsula tucked away on Point Loma in the heart of the San Diego Bay. Its namesake pier is T-shaped and only 200-feet long, but it's 500-feet wide at the end. Welcome to this small but mighty spot for fishing.

One of the best things about fishing at the Shelter Island Pier is that it's free! In fact, California law allows anyone to fish from a public pier without a license, and so anyone can enjoy this hassle-free and cost-effective option. An added bonus is that you don't even need to bring your own fishing equipment, as there's a bait and tackle shop right on the pier.

Timing your fishing trip can make all the difference. The best times to cast your line in the water are during changing tides, when nutrients are stirred up and fish come to feast. Check local tide charts to plan your visit for optimal fishing conditions. Different times of the year bring different kinds of fish, so there's always something new to catch.

You can reel in a variety of fish species from these waters, including kelp bass and sand bass, bay bass, calico bass, mackerel, barracuda, sculpin, yellowfin croaker, and herring; and the pier is equipped with everything you need for a comfortable, successful fishing trip. There are benches for relaxing, fish-cleaning stations, and lighting for those who enjoy night fishing.

Of course, fishing at the Shelter Island Pier isn't just about the catch – it's also about the views, like anything else in San Diego. Simply cast your line and soak in the stunning surroundings, catch a fish or two, and enjoy the beauty that is the Shelter Island Pier. While you wait for a bite on your hook, check out the breathtaking vistas of the bay and watch as military ships and aircraft from the nearby base glide by. There's really nothing quite like it.

Address 1776 Shelter Island Drive, San Diego, CA 92106 | Getting there By car from North Harbor Drive, turn left onto Scott Street, then left onto Shelter Island Drive. Keep right on Shelter Island Drive through the traffic circle and park at the Shelter Island Shoreline Park. | Hours Daily 6am–10pm | Tip Fathom Bistro offers tackle for those fishing from Shelter Island Pier, and they also sell house-made sausages and craft beer, all often served up by a pirate of sorts (1776 Shelter Island Drive, fathombistro.com).

39 Free Flight

Exotic bird sanctuary that educates and entertains

A place of parrot care and public education regarding our fancy feathered friends, Del Mar's Free Flight Exotic Bird Sanctuary is tucked away not-so-quietly behind the fairgrounds. Established in 1981, what began as a boarding and breeding facility has since evolved into a haven dedicated to sheltering, nurturing, and resocializing parrots. Ensuring their well-being is paramount.

One of Free Flight's aims is to understand the complex needs of these exotic birds. By prioritizing their physical, mental, and emotional requirements, the sanctuary either offers a permanent home on site or seeks appropriate places for rehoming, tailoring the approach based on each bird's individual needs. As a nonprofit organization, Free Flight's success is tied to the generous support it receives. Relying on grants, donations, memberships, and the contributions of volunteers, the sanctuary and its friendly, albeit eccentric, residents continue to flourish after more than 40 years of operation.

The sanctuary is also committed to promoting the understanding of these birds and fostering the enriching human-animal bond. Through various programs, such as yearly memberships, they raise community awareness and provide insight into these relationships. Visitors can spend time at Free Flight and enjoy a first-hand experience with the residents. While only members, staff, and volunteers are permitted to handle the birds, visitors quickly bond with the living dinosaurs by chatting up a storm and feeding them some of their favorite foods.

It's important to keep in mind that visitors are welcome by appointment only to ensure the space remains serene – but don't be fooled by the term "serene." These birds have a lot to say, and they say it loudly. While you're there, be sure to check out the koi pond, which originally served as a habitat for rescued flamingoes, who have since found homes.

Address 2132 Jimmy Durante Boulevard, Del Mar, CA 92014, +1 (858) 481-3148, www.freeflightbirds.org, freeflightbirds@live.com | Getting there Bus 101 to Camino Del Mar & 29th Street | Hours By appointment only | Tip Head to the neighboring Viewpoint Brewing Company for a pint on their lagoon-facing patio while admiring the flora and fauna of the San Dieguito Lagoon (2201 San Dieguito Drive, Suite D, Del Mar, www.viewpointbrewing.com).

40 The Front Arte & Cultura

On the border of art and community

Located in San Ysidro near the US-Mexico border, The Front Arte & Cultura is a dynamic gallery and community space dedicated to both art and cultural engagement. Established in 2007 by the nonprofit Casa Familiar, The Front is a creative and social space that provides an inclusive platform for exploring themes relevant to the border region, such as migration, identity, and social justice. By showcasing a diverse range of artwork from both emerging and established artists, The Front celebrates the unique blend of Mexican and American influences in San Diego, specifically in the San Ysidro/Tijuana area.

It's not just a regular gallery with a series of paintings to look at. Much of the work is interactive, and performances and spoken-word events offered reflect the cultural vibrancy of the community. The gallery also prioritizes educational outreach, providing workshops, lectures, and artist talks that inspire local youth and other community members.

The Front's activity and exhibitions are deeply connected to its parent organization, Casa Familiar, located in the same building, which has served the community since 1973. Casa Familiar provides essential services, including affordable housing, community engagement programs, and cultural initiatives that uplift and support underserved communities in South San Diego, especially the San Ysidro area.

Through Casa Familiar and its broader programs, The Front has become an important part of San Ysidro's cultural and social landscape, showcasing art of course, but also strengthening community bonds and providing a space where both residents and visitors can engage with the area's cultural heritage. It's a place where anyone who shows up can learn more about the dynamic relationship between art, culture, and social advocacy. Regardless of where you come from, your experience at the gallery will be an impactful one.

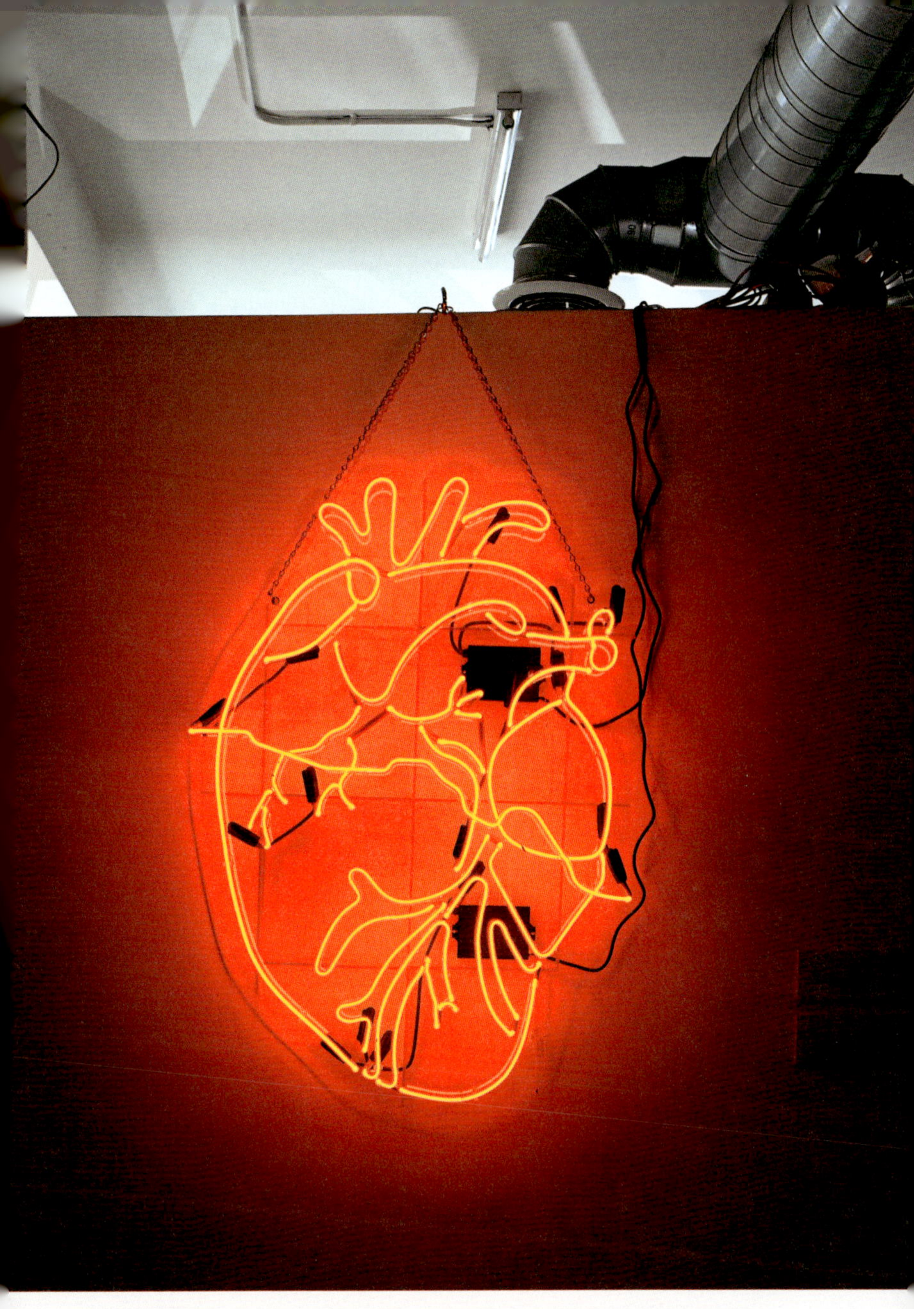

Address 147 West San Ysidro Boulevard, San Diego, CA 92173, +1 (619) 428-1115, thefront.casafamiliar.org, thefront@casafamiliar.org | Getting there Bus 907 to Cottonwood Road & Seaward Avenue; Trolley to Beyer Boulevard (Blue Line) | Hours Tue–Sat 11am–6pm | Tip Stock up on some of the city's best soft conchas, empanadas, and an incredible variety of Mexican treats at Panaderia Gonzales (475 Beyer Boulevard).

41 Fruit & Vegetable Museum

An educational detour at Specialty Produce

Surprisingly situated between the San Diego International Airport and the I-5, a perpetually busy freeway, is Specialty Produce, a San Diego gem that turns fruit-and-veg shopping into an adventure with its Fruit & Vegetable Museum. Far from your average market or grocery store, this institution is an educational showcase of global produce.

Step into the large hallway that juts off the main entrance where photographs from the team's world travels – from Tahiti to London, Germany to Malaysia – adorn the walls. Each image is both a visual treat and a portal to knowledge, thanks to embedded QR codes that connect to the Specialty Produce app or website. There, you'll dive into the world of each item's origin, culinary uses, nutritional info, and so much more. For the curious foodie, this feature is a tasty goldmine. Ever wondered how to use an ice cream bean or what to do with jering? How about the oft-forbidden fruit that is the durian? The app guides you through these exotic finds as well as local gems, like heirloom tomatoes, avocados, and a wide variety of citrus fruits.

The museum experience caters to all. Group tours are packed with interactive fun, perfect for those shopping with kids, while solo explorers can revel in a self-paced tour packed with delicious discoveries.

Specialty Produce also shines a spotlight on local goods. Rotating shelves in a window display showcase specialties from both the San Diego and Santa Monica Farmers Markets, championing Southern California growers and fresh, quality produce. What began as a supply warehouse for restaurants has transformed into a destination for both chefs and food enthusiasts, and the ability to hand-select ingredients is an experience in itself. Global and local agriculture meet here, and everyone gets a chance to explore and learn about the vast, flavorful world of fruits and vegetables.

Address 1929 Hancock Street, No. 150, San Diego, CA 92110, +1 (619) 295-3172, www.specialtyproduce.com, info@specialtyproduce.com | Getting there Trolley to Washington Street (Blue or Green Lines); bus 10 to Pacific Highway & Washington Street | Hours Daily 8am–5pm | Tip Check out the plants some of these exotic fruits come from, and even take a few home from the Exotica Rare Fruit Nursery (2508 E Vista Way, Suite B, Vista).

42 Galleta Meadows Estate

Larger than life art in the wild, wild west

Galleta Meadows Estate in Borrego Springs is a unique blend of large-scale art and desert landscape. Set within the Anza-Borrego Desert State Park, California's largest state park, this outdoor gallery spans 1,500 acres and is dotted with over 130 metal sculptures. Dennis Avery, philanthropist and heir to the Avery label fortune, purchased 3,000 acres in the early 1990s to prevent the area from being developed. He wanted to create a space here where art could be part of the open desert. He partnered with Ricardo Breceda, a self-taught sculptor, to make this vision a reality.

Breceda's path to sculpture wasn't typical. Originally from Durango, Mexico, he was a construction worker and cowboy boot salesman. He made his first creation, a life-sized T-Rex, as a promise to his daughter after she became fascinated by *Jurassic Park* and requested a dinosaur for Christmas. Using scrap metal, Breceda quickly turned his hobby into a new career. Avery commissioned Breceda to fill Galleta Meadows. Breceda created a landscape where prehistoric creatures, historical figures, and desert wildlife coexist.

The desert setting makes for an epic backdrop to Breceda's works. It's rugged and vast, with sweeping views of rocky mountains and sun-scorched plains. The environment shifts from dry and harsh to vibrant bursts of wildflowers in the spring. It's also a recognized International Dark Sky Community, where the night sky offers a clear view of countless stars.

Visitors can explore the sculptures by driving through the estate, encountering each one as it emerges from the desert floor. One of the coolest works is a 350-foot-long serpent that appears to swim through the sand, while scorpions, saber-toothed cats, and bighorn sheep seem frozen in mid-movement. There are also plenty of dinosaurs to be seen, a nod to the creatures that provided the original inspiration.

Address Visitors Centre, 200 Palm Canyon Drive, Borrego Springs, CA 92004, www.underthesunfoundation.org | Getting there By car, from Borrego Springs, take Palm Canyon Drive west to the Visitors Centre for a map of the sculptures that are spread throughout the valley | Hours Unrestricted | Tip Explore Queen Califia's Magical Circle, artist Niki de Saint Phalle's beautiful mosaic sculpture garden named in honor of Queen Califia of California, in Kit Carson Park (3333 Bear Valley Parkway, Escondido, www.visitescondido.com).

43__Garage 79

A beerlicious time capsule along the 79

It began in the 1960s as a gas station along Highway 79 in Warner Springs, back when this scenic road was a key stop for travelers heading to the hot springs at Warner Springs Resort. It was the kind of place people would pull into with a gorgeous car, the sun bouncing off polished chrome, while families and road trippers fueled up for their journeys. Even today, it's easy to imagine the station in its prime, with now-classic cars lined up, their drivers chatting and stretching their legs under the California sun – maybe because it still is that kind of place.

In early 2021, Garage 79 reopened as a craft beer bottle shop, keeping the vintage gas station feel alive with its retro signage and old-school cool vibe inside. As you drive here, the surroundings make the trip itself feel like part of the experience. Highway 79, with its tight curves, long stretches, and desert plants and animals, attracts gearheads and motorcyclists who often make Garage 79 a weekend stop. You'll likely see a great car or motorcycle parked out front regardless of the day, and the shop regularly hosts car and bike shows that draw enthusiasts from across the area.

Inside, you'll find a welcoming space for people, pups, and even UFO dwellers, with San Diego craft beers, local wines, and non-alcoholic options like kombucha and tepache on tap. The outdoor beer garden offers mountain views and a relaxed spot to enjoy food from rotating vendors serving tacos to pizza, and everything in between. Classic rock spins on vinyl, comfy seating makes you feel at home, and a primo selection of locally made snacks is sure to keep you satiated.

So if you ever find yourself along the picturesque Highway 79, make a point of visiting Garage 79, and you'll feel like you've stepped back in time. The building still embraces its history, and your taste buds will appreciate today's beer options.

Address 36651 CA-79, Warner Springs, CA 92086, +1 (760) 689-2004, www.facebook.com/theGarage79 | Getting there By car, drive CA-79 toward Warner Springs until you see Garage 79 on your right | Hours Fri 3–9pm, Sat noon–9pm, Sun noon–5pm | Tip Check out the historic Warner-Carrillo Ranch House, a former way station for emigrants on the Southern Emigrant Trail in the 19th century (29181 San Felipe Road, Warner Springs, www.sohosandiego.org/warners).

44 The Giant Dipper

The roller coaster ride of a century

Sitting pretty with its timeless structure and bright lights in Mission Beach's Belmont Park, the Giant Dipper is a tangible relic from the golden era of American roller coasters. Its tracks opened on July 4, 1925, coinciding with the opening of the park, and a century later, this wooden coaster still offers thrills – and a direct portal to the past.

John D. Spreckels (1853–1926) was a transportation and real estate mogul in the area, who played a big part in creating San Diego as we know it today. The Giant Dipper was designed by renowned roller coaster architects Frank Prior and Frederick Church, and constructed by the Sugarman Construction Company under Spreckels' vision. The coaster's architectural ingenuity and historical charm remain undiminished.

Of course, the ride itself isn't the only thing that's reached highs and lows. The coaster's history has undergone twists and turns of its own. Aside from surviving several earthquakes, the Giant Dipper was nearly destroyed by a fire in 1955, leading to the owner's bankruptcy, and its neglect in the 1970s almost saw it demolished in 1976. Luckily, a 1978 initiative led by passionate locals saved the park, resulting in a full restoration that was completed in 1990. These preservation efforts were made by a dedicated nonprofit organization, Save the Coaster Committee, which secured the Giant Dipper's future. It earned the National Historic Landmark designation in 1987, which meant that the coaster is considered to be an exceptional aspect of American culture and history. So beyond the adrenaline rush, it's also a palpable piece of early 20th-century amusement park legacy.

The Giant Dipper is no Six Flags mega-coaster. But standing at nearly 75 feet high and 2,600 feet long, and reaching speeds of 55 miles per hour, it is the heart of Belmont Park, and its generations of visitors keep that heart beating.

Address 3146 Mission Boulevard, San Diego, CA 92109, + 1 (858) 488-1549, www.belmontpark.com, info@belmontpark.com | Getting there Bus 8 to W Mission Bay Drive & Mission Boulevard | Hours See website for seasonal hours | Tip Take a dip at the nearby Plunge swimming pool, originally built in 1925 and converted from ocean water to fresh water in 1940 (3115 Ocean Front Walk, www.plungesandiego.com).

45 Goblin Shark Emporium

Shop like an O'sider

Sitting pretty along the South Coast Highway, Goblin Shark Emporium is a shop that truly thrives on the weird and creative. Owned by artist Kelly King, it's named after the goblin shark, a bizarre, prehistoric fish (just google it – you won't be disappointed), and everything about the place really does reflect Oceanside's vibe.

As soon as you step inside, the door chime meows at you (yes, meows), bringing confusion and the need to find the cat that's clearly (not) hiding out in the shop. The walls are covered in local art; murals, installations, and handmade pieces, which are all for sale and surprisingly reasonably priced.

A fuzzy TV and a shark head dominate part of the space, sharing it with vinyl records, DIY crafts, and a small section of vintage clothes, and VHS tapes. The layout is as quirky as the items themselves, and that's part of the charm here.

The shop also doubles as a creative space. Every month, a featured artist or group of artists takes over the gallery, which hosts an opening reception for them on the first Saturday. It's casual, laid-back, and a great way to meet the artists and see what they've been working on. Then, on the third Saturday of each month, the shop hosts a drink-and-craft event. It's exactly what it sounds like: grab a drink, settle in, and make something with your own hands (check their Instagram, @goblinsharkemporium for details). Whether you're a seasoned artist or just curious, these events are a fun, no-pressure way to get creative and have a great night.

Goblin Shark isn't just about selling things. It's also about celebrating Oceanside's unique, gritty, "stick it to the man" kind of energy. It's a little bit chaotic, but in the very best way. Come here whenever you're shopping for something unusual, want to get your hands on some local art, looking for a bit of inspiration, or just want to see what Oceanside is all about.

Address 109 South Coast Highway, Oceanside, CA 92054, +1 (442) 226-8216, www.goblinsharkemporium.com | Getting there Bus 101, 302, 318, 392 or 395 or Metrolink Inland, Metrolink Orange, Pacific Surfliner, or Amtrak Thruway to Oceanside Transit Center | Hours Fri–Mon 11am–6pm | Tip Take a look at the rare plant vault along with the Black Market Gallery and Oddities at Artifacts and Artichokes (7549 Mission Gorge Road, www.artifactsandartichokes.com).

46_The Gold Dust Collective

The strange, spectacled, and splendid

The Gold Dust Collective is a treasure trove for those who love the unexpected. Owners Kate Conner and Damien Ducommun have created a place where every item has a tale / tail, and nothing stays the same for long.

Tucked away on Ray Street in North Park, surrounded by coffee shops and home goods stores, the shop feels like you're walking into the attic of an eccentric collector, though with better lighting and no mothballs. It is packed with curiosities. Antique furniture hosts displays of handmade headwear from Haberdash Hats, crafted using age-old techniques meant to outlast their owners, and jewelry from Flight of Fancy, created with ethically sourced gemstones and reclaimed materials. Vintage clothing and homewares are tucked between oddities, like preserved spider webs, old poison bottles, and taxidermy with a sense of humor (think poker-playing raccoons, pole-dancing mice, and wise-looking, bespectacled skunks).

Conner and Ducommun source everything themselves, scouring online auctions and traveling to find pieces that fit their vibe. The taxidermy is particularly striking, not morbid, and oddly full of life. It's hard not to smile at a burlesque gator or the "Sassy Charlotte's Web," hand-embroidered with some colorful language. The shop's mix of macabre and playful feels deliberate, never forced, and always fresh.

The maximalist aesthetic here, paired with its ever-changing inventory, means you'll rarely see the same thing twice. This place is a curiosity-hunter's dream, with handcrafted boots, leather goods, and more for those who appreciate one-of-a-kind finds. The vibe is lighthearted, yet the craftsmanship is no joke. Every piece feels personal.

Stevie Nicks' "Gold Dust Woman" might come to mind as you browse, a nod to the beautiful, strange, and enduring. Like the song, The Gold Dust Collective makes you want to pick up some amazing pieces to take home.

Address 3824 Ray Street, San Diego, CA 92104, www.thegolddustcollective.com | **Getting there** Bus 7 to University Avenue & Grim Avenue, or bus 7 or 10 to University Avenue & Herman Avenue | **Hours** Wed–Sat 11am–6pm, Sun 11am–5pm | **Tip** Score another kind of vintage at Replay Toys Boutique, just down the street, for new and preloved toys, along with a great selection of old-school items and collectibles (3825 Ray Street, www.replaytoysboutique.com).

47_Golden Door Country Store

A taste of approachable luxury

Built out of a desire to feed the local community during the pandemic, the Golden Door Country Store mixes the luxury of the Golden Door, one of the most renowned spas/resorts in the world, with the affable atmosphere of a charming, roadside produce stand.

When the resort was closed during COVID, its farms had an abundance of fruits and vegetables that needed to be eaten. But as there aren't many markets nearby, the team at Golden Door opted to make the produce available to their neighbors. Big, five-dollar bags of oranges, still a staple item at the market, and other inexpensive fresh items were the initial offerings, soon followed by artisan breads and some non-perishables, like beans and pasta.

Today, the store carries bread from the spa's own bakery and other local bakers; a large, seasonal assortment of fruits and vegetables from both its farms and neighboring ones; and a variety of gourmet mixes, canned items, local honey and eggs; and even some handmade gifts. All items are carefully curated and reasonably priced, so sticker shock is an unlikely side effect of a visit to this charming, rural boutique.

Of course, the shop wouldn't be complete without goods from their namesake, the Golden Door. Skin cleansers, bath soaks, balms, and lotions from the spa are available, providing customers with a hint of the pampering experience without the price tag of booking a session there.

Deliciousness and skincare aside, perhaps the best quality of the store is its humanity, commitment to community, and its sustainable, biointensive farming practices. Lastly, 100 percent of Golden Door's net profits go to select charities to prevent and treat child abuse and neglect, including, but not limited to, the Rady Children's Hospital, the "I Have a Dream" Foundation, and Casa de Amparo.

Address 314 Deer Springs Road, San Marcos, CA 92069, +1 (760) 310-7573, countrystore.goldendoor.com | Getting there By car, take I-15 north of Escondido, turn west on Deer Springs Road and drive about 3 minutes to the destination | Hours Visit website for current hours | Tip Head slightly north on I-15 to take a look at the world's largest auto museum of convertibles and Americana at the Deer Park Winery and Auto Museum (29013 Champagne Boulevard, Escondido, www.deerparkmuseum.com).

48 Gossip Grill

#worldsbestladiesbar

Sitting along University Avenue in San Diego's Hillcrest neighborhood (or "gayborhood, as it's often-called), Gossip Grill is a vital part of the local area. Since opening in 2009, it's become a cherished space for the LGBTQIA+ community, particularly as one of the few remaining lesbian bars in the country and the only one in Southern California.

Lesbian bars in America have long served as critical gathering spots for women to build community, engage in activism, and find solidarity. The first lesbian bar in the US, Mona's 440 Club, opened in San Francisco in 1936. Before then, during Prohibition, other such spaces existed but were often underground and undocumented. By 1980, the number of lesbian bars had swelled to over 200 across the country. Now, only 33 remain.

The decline in lesbian bars emphasizes the importance of spaces like Gossip Grill. According to the Lesbian Bar Project, a lesbian bar prioritizes creating space for people of marginalized genders, including women (both cis and trans), non-binary individuals, and trans men. These bars aim to be inclusive of all individuals across the LGBTQIA+ spectrum, making the term "lesbian" a broad and empowering label for anyone who identifies with it.

Gossip Grill's whole vibe reflects its mission to be an inviting and inclusive space, with feminine-inspired decor, a welcoming patio, and the friendliest staff. And, while the bar is renowned for its cabaret drag brunches, bingo nights, and queer dance parties, the cleverly (oft-X-rated) named menu items are just as much fun as the entertainment.

After 2pm on weekends, Gossip Grill caters exclusively to guests 21 and over, and though the bar is open to everyone, it remains a sanctuary for the LGBTQIA+ community, offering a space where everyone can feel safe, accepted, and celebrated, and providing a haven for those who may need it most.

Address 1220 University Avenue, San Diego, CA 92103, +1 (619) 260-8023, www.gossipgrill.com | Getting there Bus 1 or 11 to University Avenue & Vermont Street, or bus 1, 10, 11 or 120 to University & 10th Avenues | Hours Tue–Thu 2pm–midnight, Fri 2pm–2am, Sat 11–2am, Sun 11am–10pm | Tip Check out the Hillcrest Farmers Market, San Diego's original and largest market, on Sundays from 9am–2pm (1601 University Avenue, www.hillcrestfarmersmarket.com).

49 Greatest Generation Walk

A walk to remember

When near the Embarcadero in San Diego, you'll see a path lined with a variety of statues and monuments. This is the Greatest Generation Walk, an homage to the legacy of the people born between 1901 and 1927. They lived through the Great Depression and fought in World War II.

Journalist Tom Brokaw coined the term "Greatest Generation" in 1998.

One of the walk's most iconic installations is the 25-foot-tall *Unconditional Surrender*. Inspired by the famous V-J Day photograph, it captures a sailor and nurse celebrating the end of WWII with an impromptu embrace. Nearby, the *Aircraft Carrier Memorial* stands in polished black granite, engraved with the names of all US Navy carriers. Bronze statues of a naval aviator and an enlisted airman stand watch, highlighting the crucial role aircraft carriers played in key battles.

The statue *Homecoming* depicts a sailor reunited with his family. This life-sized, bronze sculpture captures the joy of returning home and the sacrifices of military families, of which there are many in San Diego. It's a reminder of the strength required on the home front. Continuing along the path, the USS *San Diego Memorial* pays tribute to the storied service of the cruiser USS *San Diego* (CL-53). A bronze sailor stands beside a large bas-relief of the ship in battle, commemorating one of the most decorated ships of World War II.

One of the most unique tributes, however, is *A National Salute to Bob Hope and the Military*, which immortalizes the beloved entertainer's commitment to lifting the spirits of troops. Sixteen bronze statues depict military personnel from different branches and conflicts, gathered around the central figure of Hope (1903–2003) as if attending one of his famous, morale-boosting performances. This installation captures Hope's impact on the lives of countless service members through his decades of dedication to their well-being.

Address 43–99 Tuna Lane, San Diego, CA 92101 | Getting there Bus 923 or 992 to Broadway & North Harbor Drive | Hours Unrestricted | Tip Head to the Tuna Harbor Dockside Market on Saturday mornings to check out the freshest of catches from local fishermen (598 Harbor Lane, www.thdocksidemarket.com).

50_The Gutter

This ain't Homer Simpson's bowling alley

The Gutter bowling alley is the perfect mix of old-school charm and modern fun. Tucked under the LaFayette Hotel, this isn't your average bowling spot, but rather a carefully crafted replica of financier, industrialist, and art patron Henry Clay Frick's (1849–1919) private bowling alley at his Fifth Avenue mansion in Manhattan. Frick's 1914 alley was the height of luxury back in the day, complete with vaulted ceilings, maple and pine lanes, and stunning architecture borrowed from 17th- and 18th-century England. While his original setup can't be used anymore due to modern safety codes, The Gutter does a fine job of bringing its style and spirit back to life.

The centerpiece of The Gutter is its vintage-styled lanes, complete with a custom, gravity-fed ball-return system that's as satisfying to watch as it is to use. And there's much more than bowling to experience here. There's a solid lineup of other games, including pool, Skee-Ball, basketball, and shuffleboard, giving you plenty of options if you're more about hanging out than hitting strikes, or if the lanes are all in use.

The vibe in the space is cool without trying too hard. There is a mix of retro décor and speakeasy aesthetics, and it's a place where you'd feel equally at home wearing a tee and sandals or decked out in cocktail attire. The bar is fully stocked with beverages that go way beyond the usual beer-and-shot fare, making it just as much a place to drink as to play. And, if you're in the service industry, Mondays mean free bowling for Industry Night, which feels like a small but thoughtful perk for local workers.

Whether you're here to roll a few frames, sip a good drink, or just soak up the ambiance, The Gutter offers a fresh twist on a classic night out. It's part of what makes the LaFayette Hotel such a standout spot in San Diego: fun, a little quirky, and a place you must visit.

Address 2223 El Cajon Boulevard, San Diego, CA 92104, +1 (619) 296-2101, www.lafayettehotelsd.com | Getting there Bus 1 to El Cajon Boulevard & Alabama Street | Hours Daily 5pm–2am | Tip Get another taste of old-school cool (but definitely more laid back, O'side-style) at Surf Bowl. If you're a fan of the show *Animal Kingdom,* it was the alley owned by Joshua 'J' Cody toward the end of the series (1401 S. Coast Highway, Oceanside, www.surfbowloceanside.com).

51 Harper's Topiary Garden

A wonderland of greenery

Passing by the Harper household in Mission Hills, you'll notice that the garden in their front yard is anything but an ordinary lawn. It's Harper's Topiary Garden, and it's bursting with a variety of creatures of all shapes and sizes, much to the delight of anyone who sees it. Topiary is the practice of trimming live plants, like shrubs or hedges, into intricate and ornamental shapes, and it also refers to the plants themselves, blending creativity and horticulture. And this garden is an enchanting display of topiary art.

The private garden, created in 1994, began serendipitously when a cape honeysuckle drifted into Edna Harper's yard from next door. Inspired by this lovely shrub, Edna (aka Edna Scissorhands) and her husband Alex embarked on a visionary project to transform their green space into a magical topiary display. Alex wasn't quite sold on it at first, but with Edna's determination, Alex's support, and the help of a hard-working gardener, magic was made.

Using nothing more than simple hand tools, the couple meticulously shaped all the plants into whimsical figures that captivate and charm. Today, the garden features over 50 distinct topiaries, including elephants, whales, and figures, like dancers and a surfer, each crafted with painstaking detail and care.

The Harpers' creation is more than just a personal passion; it's a work of living art that enhances the neighborhood and brings so much joy to passersby. Though it remains part of their private residence, the couple does love how much people appreciate it. Of course, the garden is best viewed from a distance and must not be touched or disturbed as the living sculptures are fragile.

Whether you're a garden aficionado, an art lover, or anything in between, Harper's Topiary Garden is the perfect stop to see just what can be done with some creativity, dedication, and a pair of good gardening shears.

Address 3549 Union Street, San Diego, CA 92103 | Getting there Bus 10 to Washington & India Street | Hours Viewable from the outside only | Tip Make your way to the beautiful Japanese Friendship Garden, which represents the friendship between San Diego and its sister city, Yokohama, Japan (2215 Pan American E Road, www.niwa.org).

52 Hibakujumoku

Botanic Garden miracles

In the dappled sunlight of the San Diego Botanic Garden, an extraordinary story unfolds in the shape of a small tree amidst the lush foliage. It's not just any tree, however, and it comes with a message.

In the summer of 2023, the garden welcomed the remarkable addition: a seedling cultivated by scientists and botanic experts from a ginkgo tree that miraculously survived the atomic bomb in Hiroshima eight decades ago. This living relic is a participant in the Green Legacy Hiroshima Initiative, a global campaign with a noble mission: to disseminate the universal messages of caution and hope embodied by the unique survivor trees of Hiroshima.

The survivor trees, known as *Hibakujumoku* in Japanese, serve as poignant reminders of the threat of mass destruction, particularly nuclear weapons. The ginkgo, a symbol of sacred humanity and nature's resilience, is part of a global effort spanning over 40 countries. Seeds and saplings from A-bombed trees are meticulously cultivated, forming a living legacy that transcends borders and generations, with a visionary goal of a nuclear-free and ecologically sustainable planet via a long-term campaign over 1,000 years, as ginkgos often live that long.

This ginkgo arrived in the San Diego Botanic Garden in 2020 as a seedling from Shukkeien Garden in Hiroshima, and it was planted in June of 2023. Now, as people wander through the beloved 37-acre garden in the heart of Encinitas, they will get a little reminder of the message of the Green Legacy Hiroshima Initiative, spreading the word about the danger of arms of mass destruction, while celebrating the resilience of both humans and nature.

While this particular addition seems like a small change to the massive garden, which hosts over 5,300 plant species on the property, this tree is an honored ambassador of peace and endurance, common values among all living things.

Address 300 Quail Gardens Drive, Encinitas, CA 92024, +1 (760) 436-3036, www.sdbg.org | Getting there Bus 309 or 609 to Encinitas Boulevard & Quail Gardens Boulevard, walk 15 minutes | Hours Wed–Mon 9am–5pm | Tip Continue your plant exploration and head to the Palomar College campus to check out the Edwin & Frances Hunter Arboretum (1140 West Mission Road, San Marcos, www.palomar.edu/arboretum).

53 House of Pacific Relations

They can show you the world, no magic carpet needed

The House of Pacific Relations, located in Balboa Park, offers a unique cultural experience that transports visitors across the globe without leaving the city. Established in 1935 as part of the California Pacific International Exposition with the intention of highlighting San Diego's role as a cultural and trade hub in the Pacific region, the House of Pacific Relations today aims to promote multicultural goodwill and understanding.

The space consists of 33 cottages, many of which were constructed for the 1935 exposition. Over the years, the House of Pacific Relations has expanded, adding new cottages to reflect the growing diversity of the San Diego community. In 2021, nine new cottages were added. Each cottage represents a different country or culture, and they were built in various architectural styles, showcasing the heritage, traditions, and culture of their respective nations. Countries represented include China, Mexico, Germany, Italy and Iran.

Every weekend, the cottages open their doors to the public so visitors can explore the inside, interact with the hosts, and learn about different cultures through exhibits of traditional artifacts, costumes, and crafts. The immersive experience is designed to educate and foster appreciation for the diversity of global cultures. The real treat takes place on select weekend afternoons, when the House of Pacific Relations hosts lawn programs, where individual cottages present traditional performances, food, music, dance, and arts from their culture, providing a vibrant and engaging way to experience the richness of each place.

Aside from its regular hours and happenings, the House of Pacific Relations offers a variety of workshops, programs, and even language classes to not only promote cultural understanding and appreciation, but also to bridge cultural gaps and foster a more inclusive community.

Address 2294 Pan American Plaza, San Diego, CA 92101, +1 (619) 234-0739, www.sdhpr.org, info@sdhpr.org | **Getting there** FlixBus 2017 to Balboa Park; bus 7 to Park Boulevard & Presidents Way | **Hours** Sat & Sun 11am–5pm; see website for events and special programs | **Tip** For a taste of the Mediterranean, head to Balboa International Market and stock up on meat, baked goods, and a variety of premade meals (5915 Balboa Avenue, www.balboamarket.com).

54 Jacumba Hot Springs

Peak relaxation in the Sonoran Desert

This story begins with the COVID-19 pandemic. San Diego interior designer Melissa Stukel had gone out to explore the high desert, when she came upon the old Jacumba Hot Springs Resort & Spa. She had an idea. Fast-forward to October 2020, when Stukel and her close friend and work colleague Jeff Osborne and Corbin Winters acquired the property and began their new venture. They began renovating in early 2021, and by February 2024, the hotel, mineral pools, restaurant, and bar were open for business.

"We wanted the design and architecture to fit the natural landscape and feel like maybe it has always been here," Winters explains. To achieve that harmony, the team retained the original hotel's footprint and made deliberate design choices that reflected their respect for the location's past. The three pools still hold their original shapes, and everything from doors to furniture throughout the property was carefully sourced. The 20 guest rooms have each been reimagined with built-in furniture, handmade tiles, and lighting from Mexico and Morocco, along with local and vintage artwork. These elements ground spaces and create an atmosphere that feels global, yet deeply rooted in the Sonoran Desert.

The Balneology Association of North America tests and certifies the natural mineral springs; these alkaline waters have a pH of over 10 and contain a cocktail of minerals, including hydrogen sulfide, silica, and lithium, that provides an array of therapeutic benefits. The water is the perfect temperature year-round.

The purchase of the hotel also included much of Jacumba's historic main street, several homes, and public spaces, all of which have been thoughtfully integrated into the team's vision. Weekly Candlelight Sessions, hosted at the Old Bathhouse, offer live music in an intimate setting, while the restored mineral spring-fed lake is now a public amenity.

Address 44500 Old Highway 80, Jacumba, CA 91934, +1 (619) 766-4333, www.jacumba.com, info@jacumbahotspringshotel.com | Getting there By car, take either CA-94 or I-8 to Old Highway 80 | Hours See website for hours | Tip Get your UFO fixed – or just check out the fun collection of oddities and artifacts – at Coyote's Flying Saucer Retrieval and Repair, just 8 minutes northeast of the hotel (5 In-Ko-Pah Park Road, Ocotillo).

55 Knowhere Games & Comics

Find your old faves and discover new gems

Once a year, comic fanatics, cosplayers, and pop-culture lovers descend on downtown San Diego for Comic-Con. The rest of the year can be a little quiet, though. Enter Knowhere Games & Comics in San Marcos. Since 2016, when owners Mathias Lewis and Ken Slack Jr. opened the shop, it's been a haven for comic lovers and game enthusiasts.

The store was designed to fill a major gap in Northern San Diego County. Mathias, who has worked in the comics industry since 1998, saw that local shops at the time focused primarily on Marvel and DC titles, leaving fans of independent and niche comics underserved. He wanted to create a store that offered something more: a diverse selection, exceptional customer service, and a cool space for fans to gather and connect.

Knowhere features a wide range of comics, from superhero staples to independent, obscure, and self-published works you won't find at big-box stores or even many local retailers. Mathias and his team love helping customers discover new creators, stories, and genres that might otherwise fly under their radars. This dedication also extends to games, and they have an extensive selection of tabletop and board games, collectible card games, and accessories.

The store offers free gaming spaces, private rentable rooms for events, and hosts regular gatherings for fans of all ages. Whether it's creator signings, game nights, or casual hangouts, Knowhere is the perfect spot for kindred spirits to share their love of comics and games – no pricey Comic-Con tickets required.

For Mathias, Knowhere represents a lifelong passion. "I work to give other people happiness and escape," he says, and he and his team have done just that; the store is a place where staff truly care about the customers and the products they sell.

Address 125 Vallecitos De Oro, Suite J, San Marcos, CA 92069, +1 (760) 891-8333, www.knowheregamesandcomics.com, knowheregamesandcomics@gmail.com | Getting there Sprinter train to Palomar College Station; bus 304, 305, 347, 445 or 604 to Palomar College Transit Center | Hours Mon 2–8pm, Wed, Thu & Sat noon–8pm, Sun noon–6pm | Tip Check out the impressive selection of back-issue comics and graphic novels, along with some cool skateboards, at North Park's Nuclear Comics (3076 University Avenue, San Diego, www.nuclearcomics.com).

56 L. Frank Baum House

There's no place like home away from home

From 1904 to 1910, author L. Frank Baum spent his winters in Coronado to dodge the bitter cold of his home in Chicago. While those visits might not seem like a significant amount of time, his part-time residence was hugely influential in his writing career.

Baum, best known for *The Wonderful Wizard of Oz*, which was published in 1900, wrote 13 follow-up volumes, along with numerous other books, including many non-*Oz* works under various pseudonyms like Edith Van Dyne, Floyd Akers, Schuyler Staunton, and others. His final book, *Glinda of Oz*, was published in 1920 after his death in May 1919.

The author wrote at least three of his *Oz* books and four others while staying at his rental home in Coronado. The nearby Hotel del Coronado, with its grandeur and unique architecture, apparently influenced his depiction of the Emerald City in that series of books. And, speaking of the Hotel del Coronado, Baum himself designed the crown-shaped chandeliers in the hotel's Crown Room.

Known as "The Oz House," the Queen Anne-style cottage where he resided is a notable yet easily missed landmark. The modest yellow home features a wraparound porch, gabled roofs, and intricate woodwork, and if you look closely, you might even spot the face of the Wicked Witch that peers out from the side of the house. Although it's a private residence, catching a glimpse of Baum's old stomping grounds is a surreal experience and a wonderful way to imagine his creative mind at work within its walls. The winters he spent in Coronado were both a retreat and a source of inspiration that helped shape one of the most iconic fantasy worlds in literature.

In Baum's poem "*Coronado: The Queen of the Fairy Land*," published on January 13, 1905 in the *San Diego Union*, he wrote, "And mortals whisper, wondering: 'Indeed, 'tis Fairyland! For where is joy without allow. Enjoyment strange and grand.'"

Address 1101 Star Park Circle, Coronado, CA 92118 | **Getting there** Bus 901 or 904 to Orange Avenue & Park Place | **Hours** Viewable from the outside only | **Tip** Take a look at *The Wizard of Oz* glass panels made by artist Brenda Smith at the entry to the Children's Library at the Coronado Public Library (640 Orange Avenue, Coronado, www.coronadolibrary.org).

57 La Casa de las Piñatas

Supplying colorful traditions for over 30 years

San Diego is a fiesta kind of town. Each weekend, parks and beaches fill up with families and friends, sunshades are put up, and music plays. There's usually a grill or two lit up and ready to go, and there is almost always a piñata hung off a nearby tree branch.

La Casa de las Piñatas has been family-owned and operated since it opened in 1992, and by 1998, the business had expanded to four locations. In 2001, they decided to focus on the one store, closing the others and consolidating all the merchandise and operations to the current space.

The shop offers every kind of piñata you can imagine: traditional stars, pop-culture characters, and custom-made designs. They'll even make a matching stick for your piñata if you want! Whether you're looking for a small piñata or one that's larger than life, they've got you covered. Prices are affordable, and their incredible selection of Mexican candy makes filling a piñata easy – no need to head to Tijuana to shop for candy, as many people do.

Ever ready to make a party happen, La Casa de las Piñatas also rents out party essentials, like tables, chairs, and popcorn machines, and they stock snacks, like *chicharrónes* and chips, and *chamoy* sauces for drizzling, dipping, or rimming glasses to your heart's content. They sell all the accessories you'll need for a piñata party, like sticks and rope. They even offer shoe repair services on-site – not necessarily a party favor, but who can argue with expertly repaired shoes?

Fun fact: piñatas have roots in ancient China, where revelers filled clay pots with seeds for New Year celebrations. The idea made its way to Europe and then to Mexico with Spanish missionaries in the 1700s. In Mexico, piñatas blended with Indigenous traditions, like the Aztec practice of breaking pots filled with offerings for the gods. Over time, they evolved into the colorful party tradition we know today.

Address 4208 University Avenue, San Diego, CA 92105, +1 (619) 516-3841 | Getting there Bus 7 or 965 to Marlborough & Van Dyke Avenues | Hours Mon–Sat 10am–7pm, Sun 10am–1:30pm | Tip Craving Mexican treats after piñata shopping? Get your *chamango* and *tostilocos* fix at Fruteria La Costeñita (2312 Morley Street, San Diego).

58 La Jolla Leopard Sharks

Swimming with the fishes

Famed for its breathtaking beaches, rugged cliffs, and lavish homes, La Jolla's got a little somethin' else up its sleeve: leopard sharks. These beauties flock to La Jolla Shores every summer to give birth in the gentle, sun-warmed water, though they do live in the area year-round.

While leopard sharks can be found along the Pacific Coast, from June to September, La Jolla becomes a hot spot for spotting leopard sharks as they gather here in especially large numbers. This area is one of the most accessible and exciting places to observe these animals up close. The peak season arrives in late summer, when hundreds of these sleek, spotted sharks glide through the shallow surf behind the Marine Room, just off of the beach.

Why do they choose this particular spot? The water is warmest at this time of year, and female leopard sharks come to give birth here and make use of the heat to help their young develop faster. The calm, protected waters offer an ideal nursery, free from strong ocean currents and larger predators.

Despite their fearsome name, leopard sharks are anything but dangerous to humans. Growing up to five feet in length, they're known for their distinctive black spots that mimic a leopard's pattern, which helps them blend seamlessly into the sandy seabed. Their diet is equally unthreatening, consisting of small fish, crabs, shrimp, and other invertebrates. In La Jolla's protected waters, which are part of the Matlahuayl State Marine Reserve, the sharks help balance the populations of these creatures, keeping the coastal environment thriving.

So if you want to check out these beauties, you should kayak, snorkel, or simply take a dip in the clear, shallow waters of La Jolla Shores during the warmest months. Within minutes, you might find yourself surrounded by these gentle creatures, observing their mesmerizing movements just a few feet below the surface.

Address Behind the Marine Room, 1950 Spindrift Drive, La Jolla, CA 92037 | Getting there Bus 30 to Torrey Pines Road & Viking Way | Hours Unrestricted, seasonal | Tip Grab breakfast or lunch at Caroline's Seaside Café, one of a few spots that offer dining with a view right along the water (8610 Charles F. Kennel Way, www.carolinesseasidecafe.com).

59__La Mesa Secret Stairs

A workout with a view

In the Mount Nebo / Windsor Hills area of La Mesa, you'll find seven sets of secret stairs. They offer a unique urban hike through quiet residential streets that's perfect for fitness enthusiasts or those simply looking to take in gorgeous views while getting in a little workout. Two sets of the steps were built in the early 1910s, and the remainder were installed in 1927. Designed to increase foot traffic and help locals navigate the neighborhood's steep hills, the trek makes for a solid workout with a bonus: stunning views of San Diego and Mount Helix to the east.

The journey starts at the intersection of Windsor Drive and Canterbury Drive, where a daunting set of 245 stairs, interrupted by two cross-streets, leads to the top of Summit Drive. From there, you're standing on one of La Mesa's highest points at an elevation of 830 feet, providing a clear vantage point of the surrounding area. If you continue on Summit Drive, you'll find a second stairway descending 145 steps eastward toward Beverly Drive. Go up another 44 stairs, cross Pasadena Avenue, and finish with 16 final steps and a paved path to Vista Drive.

The Mt. Nebo area is named after the ridge in Jordan where Moses was said to have been granted a view of the Promised Land. The San Diego landowner, inspired by the breathtaking views, borrowed the name, and it's easy to see why. The scenic panoramas are some of the best in La Mesa, but don't forget that this is still a suburban neighborhood. The stairs wind through quiet residential areas, so visitors should be mindful of noise and respectful of the residents' privacy while taking it all in.

The La Mesa Secret Stairs have a total of 489 steps that provide a great alternative to the gym. You can trade the treadmill and gym bros for fresh air and expansive views. For a link to the full map of the stairways, visit La Mesa's website.

Address Intersection of Windsor Drive and Canterbury Drive, La Mesa, CA 91941, www.cityoflamesa.us/298/secret-stairs | Getting there Bus 852 to University & Maple Avenues. The stairs begin at the intersection with Canterbury Drive. | Hours Unrestricted | Tip Nearby La Mesa Depot Museum is the oldest building in the city, and the only remaining San Diego and Cuyamaca Railway Station around (4695 Nebo Drive, www.psrm.org).

60_La Paloma Theatre

Blending history, cinema, and community since 1928

Sitting next to the famed Encinitas sign along the 101, La Paloma Theatre is a cinema relic anchored perfectly between the past and the present. Its charming Spanish Revival architecture, designed by Edward J. Baum, fits in well with the surrounding buildings, and the nearly century-old theater exudes an old-school cool vibe that you must experience to believe.

La Paloma's history is rich and storied. In the early days of cinema, it was the first rural theater to show "talkies," motion pictures with sound. For the still-popular silent films, there was also a stage and a large organ to accompany the picture. Legendary entertainers like Charlie Chaplin and Judy Garland have performed here.

La Paloma has undergone a few makeovers over the decades and, of course, technology has changed. Even with these periodic updates, the theater still looks much like it did when it first opened, albeit showing its age a slight bit. But don't worry – that's part of the charm.

Not just a movie-goer's delight, the theater has also been a stage for musical legends (Eddie Vedder! Jerry Garcia!), plays, and, perhaps most popular, regular midnight performances of the cult classic *Rocky Horror Picture Show*, bringing the vibrant world of Rocky, Janet, and Dr. Frank-N-Furter to life. Today, the theatre continues to combine the old and the new with a curated blend of cinematic experiences. There are typically showings of both brand-new movies and timeless classics. There's always something for every film lover to enjoy, and movie marathons and back-to-back sequels are not uncommon.

As an important part of the arts community, La Paloma also hosts film festivals, such as the Banff International Film Festival, that attract budding filmmakers and cinephiles from far and wide. Regardless of whether you're a film buff or are just looking for something fun to do, make La Paloma your destination.

Address 471 South Coast Highway 101, Encinitas, CA 92024, +1 (760) 436-7469, www.lapalomatheatre.com | Getting there Coaster to Encinitas; bus 101, 304 or 309 to Encinitas | Hours See website for schedule; box office opens 15 minutes before shows | Tip For live shows in another historic spot, head north to the legendary Star Theatre, one of 17 theatres designed by William Glenn Balch in California, and the last one still open (402 North Coast Highway, Oceanside, www.startheatreco.com).

61 Lips

Time to get fabulous

Lips is where dining meets drama, and everything is served with a side of fabulous. From the moment you walk into this drag palace, you're practically glitter bombed with glamour. Chandeliers sparkle, elaborate high-heeled shoes adorn mannequin legs overhead, and, of course, there are lip motifs galore.

The queens here are the stars of the show, and they don't hold back. These performers know how to work a room, strutting in sky-high heels and delivering lip-syncs so fierce they'll have you on your feet. One moment they're channeling Beyoncé, the next they're cracking jokes that'll make you spit out your drink. Don't be surprised if you end up in the spotlight – it's all part of the fun.

Now for the food and drinks. Lips promises dinner or brunch and a show, and the menu is packed with crowd-pleasers, from indulgent entrées to desserts that are as over-the-top as the performances. And the drinks? Darling, you haven't lived until you've had a Blackout Lemonade or a Screaming Kiki. They've got cocktails with attitude, much like the queens who serve them.

Who said drag shows were a nighttime thing? Brunch at Lips is a scene all on its own. There are bottomless mimosas (and entertainers – cheeky!), champagne flowing freely, and queens who own the stage while you feast. It's bright, it's boozy, and it's a great way to kick off a weekend – or recover from one.

Naturally, the best part of Lips is the atmosphere. It's inclusive, high-energy, and unapologetically fun. The queens make you feel like part of the show, whether they're pulling you into a number or just giving you a wink from across the room. It's an awesome place to let loose, cheer loudly, and embrace the fabulous chaos of it all. So slip on something sparkly (or not – there's plenty of sparkle there to go around!), bring a couple stacks of dollar bills, and get ready for the time of your life.

Address 3036 El Cajon Boulevard, San Diego, CA 92104, +1 (619) 295-7900, www.lipssd.com | Getting there Bus 1, 6 or 215 to El Cajon Boulevard & 30th Street | Hours By reservation only | Tip Get another kind of dinner and a show at The Prestige Magic Lounge & Show Room, where everything isn't as it seems. The close-up magic will blow your mind (827 4th Avenue, www.liveattheprestige.com).

62 The Looff Carousel

54 Looff animals (sung to the tune of 99 Luftballons)

Carousels aren't just for kids, okay? Let's just get that out of the way. When there's one as beautiful as the Looff Carousel at Seaport Village, it'd be a shame to not ride it just because of your age.

Built in Brooklyn in 1895 by master carousel maker Carl I. D. Looff (1852–1918), it is one of the oldest operating carousels in the United States. It features 54 hand-carved animals, including giraffes and camels and dragons – oh, my! This menagerie-style design, with a variety of animals rather than just horses, is characteristic of Looff's elaborate craftsmanship, and each figure is uniquely detailed from the saddles to the manes, reflecting the artistic standards of the late 19th century.

Originally constructed for a park in Texas, the carousel later moved to a couple different locations, including Santa Monica and San Francisco, before settling at Seaport Village in 2004. One of its most unique features is the original band organ, which still plays vintage carousel music, so that riders (again, of any age) feel like they've gone back in time or, at the very least, as far as their childhood, if not the 19th century.

The carousel's animals are preserved with careful attention to their original design, and two horse-drawn chariots are available for those preferring to sit rather than ride on the animals. Restoration efforts over the years have kept every aspect of it vibrant, while maintaining much of its original woodwork.

Amusement ride artisan Looff was born in the Duchy of Holstein, the northernmost state of the Holy Roman Empire, now present-day Germany, and immigrated to the US in 1870. He built over 40 carousels during his lifetime, along with roller coasters, Ferris wheels, and the Santa Monica Pier. He also made Coney Island's first carousel in 1876, and continued to make more and more elaborate rides throughout the US until his death in 1918.

Address 849 West Harbor Drive, San Diego, CA 92101, +1 (619) 839-9591, www.historiccarousels.com, info@historiccarousels.com | Getting there Trolley to Seaport Village (Blue or Silver Lines); Flixbus 2017 to Downtown/Seaport Village | Hours Daily 10am–9pm | Tip Take a ride on the Dorothea Laub Balboa Park Carousel, another historic carousel, built back in 1910 in New York state (Park Boulevard at Zoo Place, www.balboapark.org).

63 Louis Bank of Commerce

The Jewel of the Gaslamp

Louis Bank of Commerce is a gorgeous example of Baroque Revival architecture that sits in San Diego's Gaslamp district. The regal building was built on the East Coast, disassembled, put on a boat, brought to San Diego, and reassembled – and that's not even the most interesting part.

The building, commissioned by shoemaker and entrepreneur Isidor Louis, was built with granite blocks from quarries back East. It was fully built to make sure everything fit perfectly before it was transported. This all happened before the Panama Canal opened in 1914, so the ship had to go all the way around Cape Horn, an arduous but necessary practice at the time. Upon arrival in San Diego, it was reconstructed to house the Bank of Commerce until 1893. Then it was converted into an oyster bar that soon became a favorite of American lawman and gambler Wyatt Earp (1848–1929).

The upper floors became the Golden Poppy Hotel, a brothel run by Madame Cora, a fortune teller whose marketing genius was ahead of its time. Madame Cora's brothel was very high-end for that day and age, catering to wealthy businessmen, politicians, and military officers. She offered discretion, which set her establishment apart from other brothels in the area. Despite the nature of her business, Madame Cora was respected for her entrepreneurial prowess within the male-dominated industry. During the day, the ladies would walk around town carrying a bag of marbles that matched the colors of their dresses. Those colors corresponded with the colors of the rooms in the brothel. Clients would take the marbles from the women and give them to Cora so she would know which room to send them to.

Nowadays, the Louis Bank of Commerce building is primarily an office property, but it remains the "Jewel of the Gaslamp". It may be a little less – ahem – colorful, but the architecture and façade are as stunning as ever.

Address 835–837 5th Avenue, San Diego, CA 92101 | Getting there Bus 215, 225, 235, 280 or 290 to Broadway & 5th Avenue | Hours Unrestricted | Tip While in the Gaslamp Quarter, check out the site of the former Grand Pacific Hotel, the only Victorian hotel of its era still located at its original site in San Diego. Today, it is the home of Lumi, an upscale Japanese rooftop restaurant by featuring acclaimed chef, Akira Back (366 5th Avenue, www.lumirooftop.com).

64 THE MAP® of the Grand Canyons

A deep dive into art and marine ecology

An extraordinary artwork in an unexpected place merges the worlds of marine science and visual arts: *THE MAP® of the Grand Canyons of La Jolla* at the Educational Plaza in Kellogg Park. This captivating, 2,200-square-foot LithoMosaic provides a rare glimpse into the underwater world just off the coast.

The mosaic features over 100 representations of local sea creatures. The shades of blue across it depict the ocean's depths and chart the course of significant underwater canyons, including the La Jolla and Scripps Canyons. The La Jolla Canyon, beginning less than 735 feet from the shores of La Jolla Beach, plunges over 650 feet deep to where it converges with Scripps Canyon. The mosaic illustrates this bathymetrical wonder, providing a visual representation of bedforms along the canyon floor. These are key indicators that La Jolla Canyon is still an active path for sediment moving from the coast to the deeper basin.

Interactivity is key here. Different panels dot the mosaic, each embedded with QR codes that unlock a world of information. Detailed species descriptions, vivid photography, and engaging multimedia content create a vision of the map's 123 featured species.

This grand mosaic in itself is a tribute to Walter Munk, esteemed oceanographer and La Jolla Shores resident. The project, led by the Walter Munk Foundation for the Oceans, honors Munk's enduring influence on marine science.

The construction process involved 24 concrete workers and was created by meticulously placing mesh sheets with tiles in reverse order, ensuring flawless alignment. At the same time, the creation of each species, executed at a studio and at the SW Fisheries Science Center at the Scripps Institution of Oceanography, made sure the mosaic turned out to be a true work of art.

Address 8277 Camino Del Oro, La Jolla, CA 92037, www.waltermunkfoundation.org/the-map, info@waltermunkfoundation.org | Getting there Bus 30 to La Jolla Shores Drive & Calle Frescota | Hours Unrestricted | Tip Those 21+ can enjoy Oceans at Night, a monthly, after-hours event at the Birch Aquarium, featuring live music, DJs, cocktails, and games (2300 Expedition Way, www.aquarium.ucsd.edu).

65 Meadiocrity Mead

From bee to bottle

What do you get when you combine ancient tradition, modern innovation, and honey? Mead!

It's the world's oldest alcoholic beverage. In fact, it predates both beer and wine by thousands of years, and at the Meadiocrity Meadery, it's experiencing a delightful resurgence.

From the very start, the founders of Meadiocrity were homebrewers turned professional, utilizing a "bee-to-bottle" philosophy that underscores their commitment to quality and sustainability. They manage their own hives to harvest top-quality honey, and they collaborate with local farmers and ranchers to source unique, California-specific nectar. This local sourcing not only supports regional agriculture, but also the honeybees and the plants they help pollinate. So each sip is a little salute to the health of the local ecosystem.

The Meadiocrity taproom is honeycomb-themed and airy, and it's the kind of space where traditional methods meet creative experimentation. While mead is generally made from fermented honey and water, Meadiocrity isn't afraid to innovate. The menu carefully labels the sweetness levels of each mead, accommodating customers who may shy away from sweeter drinks, and everything on tap is gluten-free and crafted to contain minimal residual sugar, debunking the myth that all meads are inherently sweet.

For those with adventurous palates, options range from the standard to the unexpected – think meads infused with hops, spices, local fruits, and all kinds of other ingredients that help create their unique flavors. Clearly, the mead here isn't only for traditionalists.

Aside from the honey goodness, Meadiocrity has a cozy, local vibe, hosting regular live music and game nights. You may be drawn here by the historical allure of mead or Meadiocrity's modern twist on this ancient beverage, and your visit will be a unique and undoubtedly delicious experience.

Address 1365 Grand Avenue, No. 100, San Marcos, CA 92078, +1 (760) 279-3330, www.meadiocritymead.com | Getting there Bus 347 or 445 to Las Posas Road & Grand Avenue | Hours See website for seasonal hours | Tip Head to Lost Cause Meadery, a place where a passion for mead is front and center (5328 Banks Street, Suite B, www.lostcausemead.com).

66 Meet Cute Bookshop

Where every shelf holds a love story

Located in lovely La Mesa, Meet Cute Bookshop is a beautiful store that champions LGBTQIA+ and BIPOC authors who celebrate diverse hues of love. Its range spans contemporary, historical, paranormal, sci-fi, young adult, suspense, and mystery genres, and it's a treasure trove for every romance aficionado. Regardless of what you're into, you'll find a book here to pique your interest, especially if you're enthusiastic about kissing. Diversity stands tall here, where the books' plots are woven around underrepresented characters.

If you're not familiar, a "meet cute" refers to a first encounter that sets the stage for love in rom-coms, like when John Cusack and Kate Beckinsale reach for the same pair of cashmere gloves in *Serendipity*, or when Richard Gere pays $20 to Julia Roberts for directions to Beverly Hills in *Pretty Woman*. At Meet Cute, such narratives are celebrated, no matter how far-fetched they may seem. It's an immersion into a world where love, in all its forms, reigns supreme.

The shop, however, is more than just books. You'll also find book signings, readings, and release parties. It's a place that has created a variety of book clubs, including the "Queer Romance Book Club," and the expansive "Everything Romance Book Club." Both clubs foster deep connections over shared literary passions, and both are equally awesome.

There's also a great seating area upstairs that's ideal for perusing books, if you're so inclined. Not sure what you're in the mood to read? Check out the Blind Date section of the store to pick up a book that's been crisply wrapped in craft paper with just the story basics revealed. Once you've had your fill of beautiful books, there are plenty of other bookish goodies too. Stickers, bookmarks, pins, candles, notebooks, mugs, tea, and so much more are waiting to go home with you, regardless of the kind of romance you're coveting.

Address 8235 La Mesa Boulevard, La Mesa, CA 91942, +1 (619) 439-7707, www.meetcutebookshop.com, hello@meetcutebookshop.com | Getting there Trolley to La Mesa Boulevard (Orange Line); bus 1 or 853 to Allison & Date Avenues | Hours Tue–Sat 11am–7pm, Sun & Mon 11am–5pm | Tip Stock up on unique fantasy, sci-fi, mystery, and horror books at Mysterious Galaxy (3555 Rosecrans Street, No. 107, www.mystgalaxy.com).

67_Mick Jagger's Urinal

The British Invasion (of a toilet)

Tivoli Bar in the Gaslamp District is known for many things. It's a dive bar that used to be a regular haunt of Wyatt Earp and his wife Josephine. It has been open as a saloon since 1885 and once housed an upstairs brothel that was referred to as a "boarding house" for public record purposes. And at one point, it hosted a speakeasy in the basement. One of its most blatant claims to fame, however, involves Mick Jagger doing his business.

No, not his business of being the lead singer and one of the founding members of one of the most popular bands in history, The Rolling Stones. Back in 2005, the rockstar allegedly did his business when he peed in the bathroom at Tivoli after performing a show at nearby Petco Park as part of the Stones' "A Bigger Bang" tour. Naturally, the bar decided to commemorate the occasion by installing a lips-shaped urinal along with a gold plaque and framed photo of Jagger.

Tivoli has more history beyond a rock star's bio break. It was built on land that was originally owned by Alonzo Horton (1813–1909), who developed much of the land around San Diego Bay. The long, ornate bar that is here today is the original one. It's said to have been crafted in Boston and shipped all the way around Cape Horn at the tip of South America to San Diego. They have tons of other local memorabilia and antiques displayed around the room, including the original cash register (note: it does not take Apple Pay).

So now when you go to Tivoli, whether you're just in the area or you're popping by before a show or game at Petco, you can enjoy the memorabilia, nosh on its legendary burgers and onion rings (the perfect bites to soak up the booze), knowing you're not only grabbing a drink at the historic local watering hole, but you, too, can do your business where Mick Jagger has done his. And, as far as we know, there aren't too many places where that can be done. At least not ones that involve gold plaques.

Address 505 6th Avenue, San Diego, CA 92101, +1 (619) 232-6754 | Getting there Trolley to Park & Market (Blue, Orange, and Silver Lines); bus 3, 12 or 901 to Market Street & 6th Avenue | Hours Mon–Wed noon–2am, Thu–Sun 11–2am | Tip When you go to the bathroom at Craft & Commerce or False Idol, pay attention to the voiceover on the speakers playing negative reviews of the establishments for all to hear (675 West Beech Street, www.craft-commerce.com).

68 Mission San Luis Rey

A remarkable place with a complex past

Oceanside isn't the first place that comes to mind when thinking of the California missions, but here lies Mission San Luis Rey. Founded in 1798 and known as the "King of the Missions," this is the 18th of the 21 original California Missions, which were established by Spanish Franciscans to spread Christianity and assimilate the Indigenous. It's the largest of them all and a profound symbol of the intersection between colonial Spanish history and the Indigenous cultures of the region, particularly the Luiseño people.

The architecture of Mission San Luis Rey, a mixture of Spanish and Moorish styles, is a reminder of California's colonial past, but beyond its stately façade and sprawling grounds is the story of the Luiseño people, whose history is intrinsically tied to this mission.

The Luiseño, named by the Spanish after Mission San Luis Rey, are a Native American tribe whose ancestral lands stretched across what is now Southern California. Before the establishment of the missions, the Luiseño lived in small, politically independent villages, each with its own unique culture and language. They were skilled artisans, adept at using the resources of their land for sustenance and medicine.

With the founding of the Mission, the Luiseño experienced a massive shift in their way of life. The system brought forced labor, a change in traditional living, and exposure to new diseases. Despite these challenges, they showed resilience and adaptability.

The gardens and grounds of the mission reflect the Luiseños' deep understanding and relationship with the land; its layout, including its sunken garden and *lavandería* (laundry), offers a glimpse into practices that they had to adopt during this era. As a final reminder of the complex connection between the Luiseño and the Spanish, the cemetery here marks the final resting place of both the colonizers and Indigenous people.

Address 4050 Mission Avenue, Oceanside, CA 92057, +1 (760) 757-3651, www.sanluisrey.org | Getting there By car, take Highway 76, turn north onto Rancho Del Oro Drive, and continue straight onto San Luis Rey Avenue | Hours Daily 10am–4pm | Tip Visit California's first mission, Mission San Diego de Acalá, also known as the "Mother of the Missions" (10818 San Diego Mission Road, www.missionsandiegohistory.org).

69__Ms. Peggie's Place

Where everything is small but mighty

Most things in Pacific Beach are decidedly large – the beach itself, the personalities, the *carne asada* burritos at the Taco Stand... But if you look closely enough, you'll see that there's a charming little world that defies the laws of scale and size: Ms. Peggie's Place. It's like a Home Depot crossed with IKEA and an antique shop for a real-life *Honey, I Shrunk the Kids* situation. Since its doors opened in 1980, this quaint shop has been a haven for dollhouse enthusiasts and miniature collectors alike.

Walking into Ms. Peggie's Place is like stepping into a whimsical wonderland. Each corner of the shop is brimming with mini marvels, from handcrafted dollhouses and room boxes that tell a thousand stories, to custom flooring and wallpaper that would make any interior designer swoon. The attention to detail is astounding. Tiny trim, carpet, and even lighting and electrical solutions are available, all tailored for the miniature world.

Now, this place isn't just about dollhouses and itty-bitty furniture. It's like a miniature mall, stocking everything you can think of for your tiny project. Want a Victorian-era settee or a sleek modern lamp? They've got you covered. Want to make a little fairy garden amongst your potted plants or create a delicate vignette within your succulents? You're good. Even if you're just wanting to decorate a unique cake or help your kid with a school diorama project, there's going to be something at Ms. Peggie's Place for you.

The new, old, and handmade goods at Ms. Peggie's are so special that they make the shop feel more like a gallery for miniatures than just a store. And it really isn't just a store – it's a playground for anyone who is into miniatures. It's a spot where you can let your imagination run wild, and where tiny things are celebrated big time. Seasoned collectors and curiosity seekers cannot miss going to Ms. Peggie's Place.

Address 5063 Cass Street, San Diego, CA 92109, +1 (858) 483-2621, www.mspeggiesplace.com, mspeggiesplace@gmail.com | Getting there Bus 30 to Mission Boulevard & Opal Street | Hours Wed 11am–5pm, Thu–Sat 11am–4pm | Tip Pop across the street to Leilani's Attic and stock up on Hawaiian and other Polynesian goodies (5105 Cass Street, www.leilanisattic.com).

70 Mujeres Brew House

Drink beer like a woman

In the heart of San Diego's historic Barrio Logan, Mujeres Brew House is a rarity in the oft-crowded world of craft beer. Founded in November 2020 by Carmen Favela, this dynamic brewery is not merely a place to savor artisanal brews but also a cultural nexus dedicated to uplifting women, particularly Latinas, within and beyond the craft beer industry.

Mujeres is collaboration and empowerment personified. Favela, whose husband co-founded the nearby Border X Brewing, has been involved in the beer industry for years. Upon realizing so much of Border X's clientele was women, she decided to create a women's brew club, an educational series that was thriving until the pandemic hit. While the club was on hiatus, a brewing space became vacant nearby, and Mujeres Brew House was born.

From its inception, Mujeres has been on a mission to challenge industry norms and create opportunities for women. With only about a quarter of breweries owned by women, Mujeres stands out as an all-female-run establishment, an anomaly in the craft beer world. Led by Samantha Olson, master brewer with a degree in chemical engineering and a UC Davis Brewing program grad, the brewery crafts beers that celebrate the rich ingredients and flavors of Mexican culture.

Beyond brewing exceptional beers, Mujeres Brew House is committed to fostering inclusivity and empowerment at every level, even teaching front-of-house staff to work in the brewhouse, thus empowering the women and building their confidence in the world of beer.

In addition to all the goodness that Mujeres offers beer-wise, its loading-dock-turned-beer-garden is a beautiful space with bright décor and powerful murals, and is where a multitude of events, both big and small, are regularly held. Lotería Nights, lowrider shows, paint nights, and artisan markets are more reasons to become a part of this community.

Address 1983 Julian Avenue, San Diego, CA 92113, +1 (619) 213-4340, www.facebook.com/mujeresbrewhouse | Getting there Bus 901 to Cesar E. Chavez Parkway & National Avenue | Hours Tue–Thu 4–9pm, Fri 4–10pm, Sat noon–10pm, Sun noon–9pm | Tip Make your way to Logan Avenue and pop into Por Vida for some stunning art and Mexico-inspired specialty drinks, including *dulce de leche*, *mazapan*, and mango lattes (2146 Logan Avenue).

71 Musical Bridge

A melodic walk over 25th Street

In the Golden Hill neighborhood of San Diego, the 25th Street Pedestrian Bridge is not all that special to look at. But it is definitely more than a simple crossing: it's a giant, interactive musical instrument known as the "Crab Carillon." Designed by artist Roman de Salvo and composer Joseph Martin Waters in 2003, this unique installation allows pedestrians to make music while walking over State Route 94.

The bridge features a series of brass pipes affixed along its railing, each precisely tuned to produce a specific note. When pedestrians run a stick or any other hard object along these pipes, they play a musical palindrome, or a sequence that sounds the same forward and backward, just like the movement of a crab. This theme of symmetry inspired the name "Crab Carillon." The melody, designed by Waters, is a subtle and complex composition that complements the experience of walking across the bridge and makes it a little more exciting. Unlike typical outdoor musical sculptures, the bridge's melody is built into the infrastructure itself, encouraging people to play the song and also to create their own tunes if they want to stay a while and tap on the pipes in a different order.

This fusion of art and function is a fun combo that ensures safe passage between the Golden Hill and Sherman Heights neighborhoods, and it's an invitation for people to interact with the space in a creative way. The rhythmic clinks and chimes create an ever-changing song.

This ordinary-looking bridge brings so much more to the table than expected, combining music, art, and good old-fashioned functionality. This concept of integrating art into everyday urban situations and spaces helps transform the mundane into something creative. It gives people on their commute a bit of a joyful respite and an opportunity for play and expression where they least expect it.

Address 763-799 25th Street, San Diego, CA 92102 | Getting there Bus 3 or 5 to Market & 25th Streets | Hours Unrestricted | Tip For more outdoor music, head to the Spreckels Organ Pavilion in Balboa Park, the world's largest pipe organ in a completely outdoor venue (2125 Pan American E Road, www.spreckelsorgan.org).

72__Neel's Nursery

Bringing native plants back to Southern California

Torrey Neel has long been a fixture in Encinitas, bringing her creativity, sustainability, and a love for nature into the coastal town's community. Her journey started back in the 1980s when she opened Concept Designs, a surf, skate, and reggae shop near Swami's Beach, in the space that is now Swami's Cafe. By 1991, she had launched Environgentle, a store offering eco-friendly products, like organic cotton, hemp, and biodegradable goods years before "sustainable" became a buzzword. For 17 years, Environgentle thrived and built up a loyal community of like-minded customers, until Torrey sold it in 2008.

Later switching gears, she pursued horticulture at MiraCosta College, honing her skills at Tree of Life Nursery and volunteering with organizations like the San Diego Botanic Garden. She eventually joined the board of the California Native Plant Society's San Diego Chapter, cementing her passion for native flora, and that blossomed into Neel's Nursery, her California native plant haven along Coast Highway 101 in Leucadia.

Neel's Nursery is the perfect place for anyone wanting to learn more about native gardening or those eager to reintroduce a bit of California's wild beauty into their own yards. Open weekends and Mondays, the nursery offers everything from sages and buckwheat to San Diego sunflowers. As well as being very pretty, the plants are also adapted to the unique, local climate and help sustain pollinators and wildlife.

For gardeners at any level, Neel's Nursery has seeds, gardening books, and practical advice, along with a selection of hats, tees, stickers, and knick-knacks in the little gazebo-style shop. Torrey's decades of education, experience, and genuine love for what she does make the nursery an excellent spot for a weekend detour. Whether you're working on your garden or not, it's just nice to be surrounded by plants and learn a thing or two.

Address 466 N Coast Highway 101, Encinitas, CA 92024, www.neelsnursery.com | Getting there Bus 101 to Highway 101 & El Portal Street | Hours Sat–Mon 9am–5pm | Tip Head across the street to Pannikin Coffee & Tea for a sip and a bite in what was once the Encinitas train station building. Built in 1887 and relocated to its current spot in the 1970s, the coffeehouse opened in 1980 (510 N Coast Highway 101, www.pannikincoffeeandtea.com).

73 *Neptune's Portal*

A place to express yourself

Have you ever walked by something and thought to yourself, "What in the world is that?" *Neptune's Portal* is just that kind of thing – and then some. This piece of art perched atop a mailbox on Neptune Avenue in Leucadia is reminiscent of a green sea creature (an anemone, perhaps?) with a human head-sized hole in the front. The interior is pink and glossy, not unlike the inside of a mouth or throat, and when you look inside, you'll notice the circular, shiny pattern at the back of it, along with a lotus and a tiny camera in the middle.

Jack Lampl, the homeowner and artist behind the piece, created it as interactive art for the community, hoping people in the neighborhood would take the time to stop and notice something different. Lampl, who moved to Encinitas from Oregon back in 1986, graduated from Harvard with a visual and environmental studies degree, and has spent much of his life working with nonprofits, teaching group dynamics, and using the arts to help organizations thrive.

Now, the *Portal* isn't just something to look at – it's meant for participation. The plaque on the side of the mailbox instructs visitors to put their heads in the portal, press the button, and say something – anything! – to the other side (it is a portal, after all). You can whisper a quick hello, a bit of gibberish, a confession… anything you want.

"I know this is not an easy task and not without imagined risk," says Lampl. "We are very used to limiting our experience to the more routine and to expressing the same thing over and over again." These bits are recorded and later uploaded to a website and organized by year and month for anyone to watch. While there isn't a recording limit, most videos are only a few seconds long. So, if you find yourself in the area, stop by the *Portal* and challenge yourself to be both a participant in and an observer of this piece of art.

Address 678 Neptune Avenue, Encinitas, CA 92024, www.neptunesportal.tv | Getting there Bus 101 to Highway 101 & Leucadia Boulevard | Hours Unrestricted | Tip Head down to Fault Line Park in the East Village and take a look at the "Fault Whisper"– two otherworldly, mirror-finished, stainless-steel spheres that monitor the Rose Canyon Fault System (1433 Island Avenue, www.eastvillagesandiego.com/explore/faultine-park).

74 The New Children's Museum

A place to play and create

Situated right behind the marina in downtown San Diego, The New Children's Museum is the kind of place that flips the whole "Don't Touch" museum rule on its head. Here, kids are free to climb, swing, crawl, and create. It's like a giant playground, but with a serious artistic twist. Walking in, you're met with bright colors and the buzz of kids exploring every nook and cranny, from a traveling caravan-style theater complete with dress-up supplies to a 40-foot-long slide surrounded by floor-to-ceiling murals.

One of the absolute favorites is *Whammock!*, which is basically a massive, handwoven hammock that hangs in the middle of the room, inviting kids to bounce and crawl all over its tangled loops. They don't need instructions – they just get it! For younger kids, there's Wobbleland, a toddler-friendly zone full of huge soft sculptures shaped like fruits and veggies, including a watermelon boat and an avocado see-saw. Little ones can stack, roll, or just sprawl out on these oversized play pieces and safely explore their surroundings.

What's cool about this museum is how much it respects kids as explorers and creators. Instead of walls lined with "Keep Off" signs, everything here is designed for hands-on discovery. The exhibits were created by artists who understand how kids move and play, and each installation taps into a different aspect of creativity: color, shape, texture, and pure imagination. The space also ensures every kid feels welcome. There are sensory-friendly events for children who need a quieter experience, plus workshops and seasonal activities to keep things fresh, so no two visits are the same. Adults find themselves drawn in, too, as this is a place where grown-ups can join in the fun without feeling out of place. By the time you leave, both you and the kids are happily exhausted yet refueled with creative energy.

Address 200 W Island Avenue, San Diego, CA 92101, +1 (619) 233-8792, www.thinkplaycreate.org, info@thinkplaycreate.org | Getting there Trolley to Convention Center (Green or Silver Lines); bus 11 to Front & F Streets | Hours See website for seasonal hours and events | Tip For another learning-focused experience for the kiddos, check out the San Diego Children's Discovery Museum (320 N Broadway, Escondido, www.sdcdm.org).

75_Oasis Camel Dairy

An East County ungulate experience

Situated just outside of Ramona is the Oasis Camel Dairy, established in 2002 by Nancy and Gil Riegler. The dairy offers a serene and beautiful backdrop for an encounter with its star attractions: the majestic dromedaries. Each with a unique personality, these camels are sure to intrigue and to insight belly laughs from each and every visitor.

Nancy, with her vivacious and hilarious nature, makes every visit almost feel like you're at an outdoor comedy club. Her ability to connect and joke with the crowd is less of a tour and more of a fun experience with a good friend, while giving insight into the everyday goings on of the farm and its residents. Her interactions with the animals, especially with Koalabee, a 45-year-old parrot who has been part of Nancy's life for nearly as long, are absolute highlights. Ask Nancy about their appearance together on *The Tonight Show*.

The farm itself is great for those seeking an offbeat travel experience. Visitors have the chance to feed the camels sliced apples on popsicle sticks, offering a moment of close interaction that is both educational and fun, especially if you're in the market for a camel selfie – they're pros at the duck-lips look! The apples are included with admission, but you can purchase more with a small donation. For those seeking a bit more adventure, take a camel ride for a unique perspective of the rural beauty of San Diego County.

Beyond camels, the farm has a variety of other animals and a great shop featuring camel-milk soaps, lotions, and other goods. It is, of course, important to note that this isn't just a dairy, but a refuge for sick camels or camels who can no longer be cared for by their previous owners. The animals are loved and taken care of here, and it's a place where the joy of discovery and the simplicity of nature come together, creating unforgettable memories for all who visit.

Address 26757 Highway 78, Ramona, CA 92065, +1 (760) 787-0983, www.cameldairy.com | Getting there By car, take CA-78 (Old Julian Highway) 9 miles towards Julian. The destination will be on the right. | Hours By appointment only | Tip Drive 1.5 miles east to Trumper's Honey and Fruit Shack, a roadside stand selling local raw honey, bee pollen, jam, and more (27724 CA-78, Ramona).

76__Oculto 477

Where spirits meet the soul of Old Town

Old Town San Diego is everything. It's the literal birthplace of California, with historic buildings, museums, and colorful shops that reflect the history of the area. Oculto 477, however, represents a bit of a darker corner in Old Town, sitting discreetly within Tahona, a restaurant and bar, with an entrance that feels like a ritual.

Upon arrival, you'll first inform the hostess of your reservation and then receive a rulebook. Rule No. 10, your key to entry, requires a confession: one of the seven deadly sins. It's a fitting start to an experience that blurs the line between indulgence and reverence. The space draws its name and inspiration from El Campo Santo cemetery, which holds 477 graves right next door.

Inside, 477 lights illuminate the intimate setting, each representing a grave and bringing attention to the past. Its design leans into the proximity to the cemetery and creates an environment that feels deliberate – and just a bit spooky – without losing its charm.

The cocktails here are as much about chance as choice. While you can select from a curated menu of creative drinks, try being adventurous and let the bartenders take charge of mixing up something custom for you. Leave the fate of your taste buds in their capable hands.

The drinks menu nods to the bar's surroundings, with options like the "Garden of Death," a blend of mezcal, Alma Tepec chile liqueur, and *mole* bitters, or the "Oculto Zombie," a potent mix of rums, falernum, and absinthe.

The atmosphere is deliberately low-lit, with a speakeasy vibe that complements the cemetery's quiet presence next door. Every element, from the lighting to the drink offerings, is designed to acknowledge the spirits, whether those of mezcal or the 477 lives memorialized outside. The experience is unpretentious, and each detail stands on its own without distraction from ghosts or anything else.

Address 2414 San Diego Avenue, San Diego, CA 92110, +1 (619) 255-2090, www.oculto477.com | Getting there Bus 83 to Juan & Harney Streets | Hours Daily 5pm–midnight, reservation required | Tip Go on an interplanetary adventure at Mothership, a South Park speakeasy that brings retro and futuristic together, and is staged as the crash-landing site of a spaceship (2310 30th Street, www.mothershiptrip.com).

77 The Old Blockhouse

A legacy of war and science

The nondescript building, known locally as the "Old Blockhouse," is a US Army command post from the World War II era. This fortress-like structure, now owned by the Scripps Institution of Oceanography, played a crucial role during the war. Positioned 800 feet above sea level, it provided an ideal lookout for potential Japanese attacks following the attack on Pearl Harbor. Today, the best view of the Blockhouse is from the west side of the lawn at Mount Soledad Memorial Park.

At the outbreak of the war, the building was reinforced with concrete and steel, up to 18 inches thick at its base, and the windows were cemented over for enhanced defense. A new, innovative air-intake system was capable of drawing fresh air from 100 feet away. The Blockhouse held multiple rooms and offices extending across two underground levels, and it functioned as a communications center linking military bases across the Pacific.

In 1966, the property underwent a significant transition. Scripps constructed the first microwave antenna adjacent to the Old Blockhouse, marking the beginning of a new era of scientific exploration. That same year, the Scripps Radiocarbon Lab was established next door, led by Dr. Hans Suess (1909–1993), a German nuclear physicist and one of the founding UCSD faculty members. Suess' work focused on carbon-14 distribution in oceans and the atmosphere, and was critical in the field of nuclear physics. The lab ceased operations in 1994.

During the lab's decommissioning, Scripps scientist Jeff Bada (1942–2024) found a vial labeled in German, later identified as heavy water, a key component in nuclear reactions. This WWII vial was linked to Dr. Suess, who studied heavy water for its potential in mass-producing nuclear weapons, a project of interest to Nazi Germany. The vial, originating from Norway and kept by Suess for sentimental reasons, was handed over to the Department of Defense.

Address 7110 Via Capri, La Jolla, CA 92037 | Getting there By car, take La Jolla Scenic South Drive, and turn left onto Via Capri. The building is on the left. | Hours Viewable from the outside only | Tip Take in the monument and views, and read American veterans' stories at the nearby Mount Soledad Memorial Park (6905 La Jolla Scenic South Drive, La Jolla, www.soledadmemorial.org).

78 Palomar Observatory

To infinity and beyond!

Sitting northeast of San Diego atop Palomar Mountain is an astronomical observatory that houses the famed, 200-inch Hale Telescope, named after American astronomer George Ellery Hale (1868–1938). Construction of the observatory began in 1936 but was delayed because of World War II. It was not completed until 1948, and for nearly half a century, Hale was the most significant telescope on the planet.

The Hale Telescope was funded by a grant to the California Institute of Technology (Caltech) from the Rockefeller Foundation's International Education Board in 1928. The Corning Glass Company produced the Pyrex mirror blank for the telescope (yes, the same glass company as CorningWare® and Pyrex baking dishes). At that time, the mirror blank was the largest piece of glass in the world.

While it is no longer the site of the world's most powerful telescope, the Palomar Observatory is still an incredible place to visit. It undergoes constant upgrades to ensure that it is outfitted with state-of-the-art technologies. There's a visitor center/museum that's both kid- and pup-friendly, and boasts a wealth of information for anyone who is even slightly – or astronomically – interested in space.

A little further down the path from the Visitor Center is the Visitors Gallery, where you can actually see the Hale Telescope. One side of the area is occupied by a full-length window that provides a direct view of the telescope, and more information is available along the opposite gallery walls.

On weekends from April to October, there are guided tours of the Hale Telescope, and tickets can be purchased in the gift shop for a nominal fee. During the winter while the tours are on hold, a series of free talks take place in the visitor center, bringing the fascinating research and history to the public. These talks are hosted by Observatory staff, visiting astronomers, or docents.

Address 35899 Canfield Road, Palomar Mountain, CA 92060, sites.astro.caltech.edu/palomar | Getting there By car, take Highway 76 to South Grade Road and take Canfield Road/South Grade Road to the Observatory parking lot, and walk the marked path to the visitor center/museum/gallery | Hours Daily 9am–3:30pm | Tip Stroll the scenic Observatory Trail and sleep under the stars at the Observatory Campground, just outside the Observatory grounds (Highway S6, State Park Road, No. 21485, Palomar Mountain, www.recreation.gov/camping/campgrounds/233300).

79__Rady Shell Open Rehearsals

A behind-the-scenes look at the Symphony

The San Diego Symphony, one of California's oldest orchestras, has been essential to the city's cultural scene since 1910. With Rafael Payare as its music director, the Symphony offers a wide range of performances, from classical masterpieces to contemporary favorites. They've paired with current artists like the Violent Femmes, played movie soundtracks like *Harry Potter*, and paid tribute to favorites like Carole King and Aretha Franklin. It's been a huge part of San Diego's artistic landscape, and people from across the region come to enjoy programs that appeal to all ages and tastes. It's been especially memorable since the opening of the Rady Shell venue at Jacob's Park in the summer of 2021.

For those who are curious about what happens behind the scenes, the Symphony's open rehearsals at the Shell provide a unique window into the creative process. Visitors can observe the musicians fine-tuning their performances while enjoying the stunning bayside setting. Open rehearsals are typically accessible during public park hours, though some sessions may be closed when the venue goes into concert mode. Either way, the park's design ensures that you can still enjoy the experience from nearby.

If you're just passing through, the promenade encircling the Rady Shell offers a chance to hear the music without stepping inside. The acoustics of the venue allow the sounds to carry beautifully, creating an impromptu listening experience for anyone strolling by.

For a different perspective, head out onto the San Diego Bay. The venue's waterfront location makes it a great spot for boaters, kayakers, and paddle boarders to soak up the performances. It's a scenic and memorable way to enjoy live music against the backdrop of the city skyline.

Address 222 Marina Park Way, San Diego, CA 92101, +1 (619) 235-0804, www.theshell.org, info@sandiegosymphony.org | **Getting there** Trolley to Convention Center (Green Line) | **Hours** See website for schedule | **Tip** Book a room at Humphreys Half Moon Inn on the night of a concert you want to attend and ask for a room that backs onto the concert venue. You'll get a great view of the show from the comfiest seats around. It'll be BYOB, and you don't have to worry about driving (2303 Shelter Island Drive, www.halfmooninn.com).

80__Roberto's Taco Shop

Origin of the burrito, San Diego's official grub

Few things are more disputed in the world than the origin of the California Burrito. Okay, just in San Diego, but you get it – it's a point of contention around here. The passion for the subject makes sense. After all, it is a glorious, giant flour tortilla packed with *carne asada* (marinated, grilled steak), guacamole, pico de gallo (fresh salsa made with ripe tomatoes, white onion, jalapeños, cilantro, lime, and salt), cheese, sometimes sour cream, and the pièce de resistance: French fries.

There's a lot of debate about where the California Burrito truly originated. Of course it was here in San Diego, but which Mexican restaurant is responsible for this delicious, almost obscene invention? The general consensus says it was at one of the "-berto's" restaurants back in the 1980s. The Fresh MXN chain, formerly Santana's, has claimed responsibility, but Roberto's Numero Uno seems to be the strongest contender.

The original location of Roberto's was founded back in 1964 by Roberto Robledo and his wife Dolores. They immigrated to California in the '50s, and later started making tortillas to sell to the public, including the US Border Patrol agents who worked at an immigrant holding facility in the area.

Fast-forward a few years, and the Robledo family opened several quick-service Mexican restaurants. They named them Roberto's Taco Shop and became one of the first taco chains in the country. Over the years, more family and friends immigrated to the US, and they opened up more taco shops using the "-berto" name (keep your eye out for Rolberto's, Alberto's, Filiberto's, Jilberto's, and more), and the concept of Mexican fast food took off. The California Burrito popped up some time in the 1980s, likely from Roberto's Numero Uno, followed by Carne Asada Fries (apparently from Lolita's Mexican Food), which are basically deconstructed California Burritos, sans tortilla, in the '90s.

Address 1406 Highland Avenue, National City, CA 91950, +1 (619) 336-0741, www.robertostacoshop.com | Getting there Bus 949 to Highland Avenue & 14th Street | Hours Open 24 hours | Tip After you're burritoed out, try the Carne Asada Fries at the original Lolita's Mexican Food (413 Telegraph Canyon Road, Chula Vista, lolitasmexicanfood.com).

81 Roberts Cottages

A cozy stay right on the beach

Roberts Cottages in Oceanside are a well-preserved part of the city's beachfront history, and they're darn cute, to boot. Built in 1928 by A. J. Clark and designed by the Whiting-Mead Company, the 24 stucco cottages were originally marketed as "Clark's Cottage DeLuxe." They provided affordable, compact accommodations for beachgoers for daily rental rates starting at $3. This was a great idea then, as people from all over wanted to spend time beachfront in the glamorous coastal town.

In 1941, Harry and Virginia Roberts purchased the property and made several updates, including painting the exteriors, adding outdoor flowers, and modernizing the interiors. The cottages were then renamed Roberts Cottages, a name that has stuck around since. By 1957, the cottages transitioned to individual ownership, one of the earliest examples of the condominium concept in California. At the time, beachfront units sold for $5,950, and second-row units were priced at $5,250.

Today, the cottages remain individually owned, and many are even available as short-term vacation rentals. Their location on The Strand, just steps from the beach, makes them the perfect spot for visitors seeking a simple, beachside stay. The cottages' small size and pastel-colored façades are unique along Oceanside's coastline, now mostly occupied by large homes and hotels.

As one of the last surviving examples of auto-court beach cottages, Roberts Cottages hold a unique place in Oceanside's history. They're from a time when coastal tourism was becoming accessible to more people, and small, practical accommodations were in demand – a big change from today's more common, pricey, and large beach rentals. They're a rare and timeless piece of California's coastal culture, and whether you view them as a historical landmark or a charming vacation option, they're the ideal place to chill, beachside.

Address 704 The Strand North, Oceanside, CA 92054, +1 (760) 721-8128, www.robertscottages.com | Getting there By car, take the Pacific Coast Highway to Surfrider Way. Turn right, and the cottages will be on the right-hand side in just over one block. | Hours Viewable from the outside only; contact for reservation | Tip For more cottages from another time, visit Redwood Hollow, a set of historic bungalows built in 1915 (256 Prospect Street, La Jolla, www.redwoodhollow-lajolla.com).

82 The Salk Institute

A space for research and reflection

The Salk Institute for Biological Studies, perched atop the bluffs over Blacks Beach in La Jolla, is a gorgeous work of modern architecture designed by Louis Kahn (1901–1974), completed in 1965. Commissioned by Dr. Jonas Salk (1914–1995), creator of the polio vaccine, the Institute was envisioned as a space that would foster collaboration and innovation among scientists, while also being visually pleasing and inspiring.

Kahn's design includes 29 separate buildings that are connected to form the two main laboratory wings. These wings, constructed primarily of poured concrete, run parallel to each other, separated by a central open courtyard. The modular design of the buildings allows for flexibility in the arrangement of laboratory spaces in order to meet the changing needs of the researchers. Even changes in airflow, water lines, and light can be accommodated. The choice of concrete was intended to provide both durability and a sense of permanence, while teakwood window frames offer a natural contrast and help regulate light within the spaces.

The open courtyard is breathtaking, paved with travertine and divided by a narrow water channel, often referred to as the "River of Life," that runs down its center. The channel visually extends toward the ocean, symbolizing the flow of ideas and knowledge. Of course, natural light is central to Kahn's design. The labs face west, allowing sunlight to flood the spaces throughout the day. The large, floor-to-ceiling windows further maximize the light.

Salk played a pivotal role in the development of the Institute's design. After his success with the polio vaccine, he wanted to create a research facility that was as functional as it was beautiful. Working closely with Kahn, he ensured that the design would serve the needs of the researchers while also creating a peaceful atmosphere for their work.

Address 10010 N Torrey Pines Road, La Jolla, CA 92037, +1 (858) 453-4100, www.salk.edu, tours@salk.edu | Getting there Bus 101 to N Torrey Pines Road & Torrey Pines Scenic Drive | Hours Scheduled tours only; reservation required | Tip Make your way down to Blacks Beach and take a look at the La Jolla Mushroom House, otherwise known as the Bell Pavilion House. It was built in 1965 for Sam Bell, of Bell's Potato Chips and General Mills (9036 La Jolla Shores Lane, La Jolla).

83__San Diego Central Library

A reading room with a view, and then some

There are few better places to get some peace and quiet than a library. The hushed tones, the smell of books, and the sheer amount of knowledge that surrounds you are inspiring, to say the least. The San Diego Central Library is no exception. It exemplifies and promotes the city's commitment to literacy and community, but it is also an architectural masterpiece. And at its heart, it is just a lovely place to be.

The eighth-floor Helen Price Reading Room, specifically, offers an especially serene retreat. This space lies directly beneath the library's iconic dome, a striking lattice structure that adds to the city's already stunning skyline. The dome's intricate design shades the glass walls and ceiling, tempering San Diego's abundant sunlight and allowing dappled light to spill into the room. This soft, natural illumination makes for a tranquil atmosphere and creates a lovely environment for reading, working, or just some quiet reflection.

The floor-to-ceiling windows in the Reading Room also frame the sweeping views of the San Diego Bay, the Coronado Bridge, and the downtown area. The combo of the structure's clean lines with the expansive vistas creates an indoor-outdoor feeling, connecting both settings seamlessly, and the architectural balance continues in the room's interior, which predominantly features warm, wooden finishes and minimalist furniture, designed to encourage focus and comfort.

The ninth floor, which surrounds the Reading Room, is perhaps the liveliest area of the Central Library because it features a sculpture garden, a glass walkway, a rare-book room, special collections, and a variety of terraces that provide great views of the city. It's a welcome juxtaposition that illustrates the library's dual purpose of providing a space for introspection and learning, while also encouraging socializing and a sense of community.

Address 330 Park Boulevard, San Diego, CA 92101, +1 (619) 236-5800, www.sandiego.gov/public-library/central-library | Getting there Trolley to Park & Market (Blue, Orange or Silver Lines); bus 12, 901 or 929 to 11th Avenue & K Street | Hours Mon & Tue 11:30am–8pm, Wed–Sat 9:30am–6pm, Sun 1–5pm | Tip Check out the WNDR Museum, an immersive art experience for people of all ages (422 Market Street, www.wndrmuseum.com/location/san-diego).

84 San Diego Circus Center

No fiery hoops or lions required

Have you ever felt the urge to try your hand at circus arts? Not like Krusty the Clown or any of his other questionable pals, but the real deal. If so, the San Diego Circus Center is a place where you can run away and join the circus, at least for a little while.

With classes in aerial silks, trapeze, trampoline, tumbling, clowning, and dance trapeze, there's something for everyone, whether you're new to circus arts or have some experience. You can learn to juggle, work on acrobatics, or even just practice a handstand. The center offers both recreational programs for people looking to have fun and preparatory courses for those aiming to join top circus schools.

Jean-Luc Martin, the founder, has had a career full of twists and turns. Born in Louisiana, he moved to Quebec as a kid and got into rock climbing during college. Summers with Outward Bound introduced him to teaching and working with people, and in his downtime, he started juggling and walking the wire. His first real encounter with the circus came in 1987 when he saw *Cirque du Soleil* and decided he wanted to be a part of it.

That goal took him to San Francisco, where he joined the Pickle Family Circus and became a lead performer in aerial cradle. Later, he trained at Montreal's National Circus School, which led to his performing with *Cirque du Soleil* (the dream!) and other shows in Europe. After a stint in Hollywood working in TV and film, Martin moved to San Diego with his wife and kids, eventually finding his way back to teaching circus arts. What began as casual coaching grew into the San Diego Circus Center.

Today, the center draws students from around the world, while welcoming locals who simply want to give circus arts a try. Martin and his wife Mara run the center together, offering everything from beginner-friendly classes to intensive training programs in a community-focused space.

Address 2050 Hancock Street, Suite A, San Diego, CA 92110, +1 (619) 487-1239, www.sandiegocircuscenter.org, info@sandiegocircuscenter.org | Getting there Bus 10 to Pacific Highway & 4137 | Hours Mon–Fri 9am–7pm, Sat 9am–1pm; see website for class schedule | Tip Want to take your aerial skills a little further with aerial yoga and circus arts for all ages? Take a class or two at Aerial Revolution (4818 Ronson Court, www.aerialrevolution.com).

85_Sea Hive Station

They've got gadgets and gizmos aplenty

Sea Hive Station is not your typical antiques store. It's essentially an antique mall, but with a fresh, modern twist that makes it an epic spot for unique finds. Located in a former Naval Training Center building, this 23,000-square-foot marketplace brings together over 150 vendors offering a mix of vintage, retro, artisan, and just plain cool items.

As soon as you step into Sea Hive, you'll feel like you're on a curated treasure hunt. Every corner reveals something different: stacks of vintage vinyl LPs, racks of retro clothing, and cases of eye-catching costume jewelry that are a throwback to another decade. Collectors will find shelves lined with old-school barware, quirky collectibles, and even local honey sourced from nearby beekeepers. For the stationery-obsessed, there's an entire section devoted to unique paper products, alongside a range of hats that cater to every style, from classic fedoras to retro-glam sun hats.

If you're around for Rack-O-Rama, held on the third weekend of every month, you're in for a treat. The loading dock becomes a hotspot for vintage clothing, with racks of fashion finds from various decades. The best part? Most items are under $20! It's a go-to for vintage lovers hunting for affordable pieces to give their wardrobe a pop of character.

And on the second Sunday of each month, Sea Hive brings even more excitement with its outdoor Vintage & Makers Market. This lively event fills the parking lot with additional vendors, live music, and food trucks, making for the perfect spot to shop, snack, and spend a day outdoors, all while stocking up on great items at even better prices.

With its commitment to supporting local artisans and small businesses, Sea Hive Station is so much more than a place for a shopping trip – it's also a spot that makes you feel good about buying something unique that you didn't know you needed.

Address 2750 Dewey Road, No. 103, San Diego, CA 92106, +1 (610) 310-5099, www.seahivestation.com | Getting there Bus 28 to Rosecrans Street & Roosevelt Road | Hours Daily 11am–6pm | Tip While you're in the mood for vintage wear, head up to North County's Captain's Helm for an incredible selection of clothes and a cup of delicious coffee from their onsite coffee shop (1832 South Coast Highway, Oceanside, www.captainshelm.com).

86 The Self-Realization Fellowship

Meditate, explore, and reflect

Overlooking the iconic Swami's Beach in Encinitas, the Self-Realization Fellowship Encinitas Ashram is a tranquil, 17-acre retreat that combines meditation, education, and space to reflect. Established in 1937 by Paramahansa Yogananda (1893–1952), author of the spiritual classic *Autobiography of a Yogi,* the ashram is a serene escape and an inspiring destination for both spiritual seekers and curious travelers alike.

At the heart of the ashram are its Meditation Gardens, a beautifully landscaped space featuring a stunning variety of trees, plants, and flowers, many originally planted by Yogananda himself. Winding paths lead visitors past koi ponds, miniature waterfalls, and secluded benches, ideal for taking in your surroundings or even hunkering down with a book while subconsciously breathing in the sound of the waves below. The centerpiece of the gardens is the Ming Tree, a Monterey pine cultivated as a large bonsai, perched above the ocean. This tree, along with ancient Aleppo pines, African coral trees, and other exotic flora, reflects the thoughtful care that has gone into creating a space designed for stillness and reflection.

The Hermitage, Yogananda's former home, is another highlight of the ashram. This is where Yogananda spent much of his time writing, meditating, and hosting influential figures from around the world. For those interested in his teachings, the nearby Encinitas Temple serves as a spiritual space, offering meditations, classes, and services that introduce visitors to his philosophy of uniting East and West through the practice of yoga and meditation.

The Self-Realization Fellowship Encinitas Ashram offers a rare chance to step away from the noise of modern life, and find peace in a setting as inspiring as its history.

Address 215 W K Street, Encinitas, CA 92024, +1 (760) 753-5353, www.encinitastemple.org/visiting | **Getting there** Bus 101 to Highway 101 & K Street | **Hours** Gardens: Tue–Sat 9am–5pm, Sun 11am–5pm | **Tip** Take in the stunning architecture and beautiful Buddhist practices at Wat Lao Buddharam (726 44th Street, www.watlaobuddharam.net).

87__Sew Loka

Fashion that speaks

Sitting just a block away from the cultural heart of Barrio Logan, Chicano Park, Sew Loka is as colorful and lively as the neighborhood it calls home. The shop's black, white, and bubblegum-pink exterior sets the tone for what's inside: stacks of colorful fabric, countless spools of thread, rows of sewing machines, and a buzz of creativity you can actually feel. And, at the heart of it all is Chicana fashion designer Claudia Biezunski-Rodríguez, a woman who is clearly talented and also beams kindness.

Biezunski-Rodríguez's passion for sewing started from the get-go. She grew up in her parents' denim factory, surrounded by fabrics, patterns, and the constant hum of sewing machines. Her mother taught her how to sew and make her own patterns, skills she used early on to repurpose thrifted finds into unique outfits for her dolls.

That ingenuity is still her signature today. At Sew Loka, nearly everything is made from recycled materials; secondhand fabrics, donated textiles, or scraps that might otherwise be discarded end up as one-of-a-kind garments and accessories. In fact, the shop has earned a reputation as one of the most eco-friendly businesses in the nation, according to Yelp, a distinction that aligns perfectly with Biezunski-Rodríguez's attitude toward sustainability.

Her designs are bold and unapologetic, often embellished with words like "Chicana" or "Chingona," celebrating her heritage with style and a general tone of badassery. Some pieces incorporate intricate embroidery, patchwork, or images of the Virgin Mary, blending cultural pride with telltale artistic detail. Everything she makes feels personal and intentional.

Of course, Sew Loka is a great place to shop, but it's also where Biezunski-Rodríguez shares her craft through sewing workshops, bringing together people who want to learn or create something meaningful of their own.

Address 2113 Logan Avenue, Suite B, San Diego, CA 92113, +1 (619) 693-4964, www.sewloka.com, claudia@sewloka.com | Getting there Trolley to Barrio Logan (Blue Line); bus 901 to National Avenue & Cesar E Chavez Parkway | Hours Wed–Sat noon–6pm, Sun noon–4pm; see website for class schedule | Tip While you're in the area, walk through Chicano Park to check out the largest collection of Chicano murals in the world (1949 Logan Avenue, www.chicano-park.com).

88_South Bay Drive-In Theatre & Swap Meet

A blast from the past

Is there anything that screams summer nights more than catching a movie at a drive-in theater? Luckily, in San Diego it's basically always summer, which means the drive-in experience is available year-round.

The South Bay Drive-In Theatre & Swap Meet in south San Diego has been showing feature films since 1958. It originally had a single screen, but as its popularity grew, it expanded to three screens in the 1970s. Today, it combines old-school charm with modern touches, like digital projection introduced in 2013 for a clearer picture, and FM-transmitted audio that lets moviegoers enjoy quality sound directly through their car radios. Back in the 1950s and '60s, drive-ins were so popular, there were over 4,000 of them in the country. Today, there are only around 330 of them left, so this place is truly special. If only there was also a 1950s-style soda shop on site for a real throwback!

Another perk of the theater is its affordability. Tickets for an evening at the drive-in are just $10 for adults and $1 for kids, often for a double feature! The snack bar (cash-only, no bills over $20) keeps it classic with popcorn and candy, and also serves up carne asada nachos – could it even be a San Diego gem without some sort of *carne asada* menu option? Be sure to arrive hungry and on time. Even better, rock up at least an hour before showtime to get a prime parking spot and snacks before the first movie. On Wednesdays, Saturdays, and Sundays, the property transforms into a swap meet. Around 300 vendors offer everything from antique finds and vintage clothes to unique collectibles and handmade goods. Since launching in 1977, the swap retains a relaxed vibe that encourages browsing and mingling. It's the perfect spot for anyone who loves the thrill of a good find.

Address 2170 Coronado Avenue, San Diego, CA 92154, +1 (619) 423-2727, www.southbaydrivein.com | Getting there By car, take I-5 to Exit 4 Coronado Avenue. Turn right onto Coronado to the destination on the right. | Hours See website for showtimes; swap meet Wed, Sat & Sun 6am–2pm | Tip Keep the shopping spree going at the Spring Valley Swap Meet, San Diego County's largest outdoor market (6377 Quarry Road, Spring Valley, www.springvalleyswapmeet.net).

89_South Bay Salt Works

Stay salty, San Diego

South Bay Salt Works is the second-longest-running business in San Diego (the first is *The San Diego Union-Tribune*), operating since the 1870s. At first, it was known as La Punta Salt Works, and it quickly became the sole supplier of salt for Southern California. In 1902, the operation was purchased and renamed the Western Salt Company, which grew to become the second-largest salt producer in California throughout the 20th century.

The salt works have made the most of San Diego Bay's unique conditions, where warm, dry weather and Pacific seawater allowed for large-scale solar evaporation, the natural process used to extract the salt. It's one of the few places on the West Coast, along with the San Francisco Bay, where salt could be produced in this way. By the late 1990s, however, industrial salt production was no longer as in demand as it once had been. In 1999, the site was sold to the County Regional Airport Authority and eventually transferred to the US Fish and Wildlife Service.

Today, the salt ponds are part of the San Diego Bay National Wildlife Refuge. Although they continue to operate on a smaller scale than previously, the focus has shifted toward conservation. The high salinity of the ponds creates an ideal habitat for brine flies and shrimp, which in turn support a variety of bird species. Ninety-four species call the area home, and seven of them, including the endangered California least tern and the western snowy plover, are protected within the refuge. In 2011, two of the salt ponds were restored to natural marshlands to further enhance the ecosystem.

While the salt works itself is not open to the public, the surrounding refuge offers views of the ponds and mounds of salt, making for a pretty cool backdrop for a stroll or bike ride along the bay. If you're lucky, you might even catch a glimpse of the resident flamingo and other beautiful birds.

Address 1470 Bay Boulevard, Chula Vista, CA 91911, www.sunnycv.com/history/exhibits/salt.html | Getting there By car or bike, from Coronado go south on Silver Strand Boulevard. You can view the salt works from your bike on the Bayshore Bikeway, which has an entrance nearby. | Hours Unrestricted | Tip Get your fill of wildlife by the bay at the Living Coast Discovery Center (1000 Gunpowder Point Drive, Chula Vista, www.thelivingcoast.org).

90 The *Star of India*

She's more than just a pretty ship

If you've ever strolled along the Embarcadero in downtown San Diego, you've seen the *Star of India*. It's a gorgeous, 19th-century ship that has a fascinating history. Today, it is open to the public daily and continues to sail, making it the oldest active sailing ship in the world.

Built in 1863 at the Ramsey Shipyard on the Isle of Man, the *Star of India*, originally known as *Euterpe*, after the Greek muse of music and poetry, is one of the oldest iron-hulled merchant ships still afloat. She was designed for the bustling India trade route, and embarked on countless voyages around the world. She transported both cargo and passengers, and she even hauled workers and supplies far north for the Alaska Packers' Association.

Of course, with such an impressive history come difficulties, and the *Star of India* has certainly weathered her share of storms. In 1906, the ship survived a near-sinking incident after a collision and later endured a severe cyclone in the Indian Ocean. Sailors aboard were deeply superstitious, and tales of hauntings and ghostly apparitions were common.

Her fame also includes being involved in one of the world's longest voyages, circumnavigating the globe for nearly 21 months. She has had multiple name changes and has starred in various films and documentaries. After years of service and exciting travels, the *Star of India* was retired in 1926 and unfortunately fell into disrepair. The Maritime Museum of San Diego acquired the vessel in 1957, when she underwent a full restoration.

Today, the ship is part of the museum, and with a single ticket, you can not only check out the *Star of India*, but you can also go aboard all of the historic ships that are part of the Maritime Museum. For a small additional fee, you can take the 45-minute Narrated Historic Bay Cruise, which departs several times per day. And you don't even have to swab the poop deck.

Address 1492 North Harbor Drive, San Diego, CA 92101, www.sdmaritime.org, info@sdmaritime.org | Getting there Coaster and Trolley to Santa Fe Depot (Blue or Green Lines); bus 280, 290, 923 or 993 to N Harbor Drive & Ash Street | Hours Daily 10am–5pm | Tip Dive into more recent ship history at the USS *Midway*, the longest-serving aircraft carrier of the 20th century (910 North Harbor Drive, www.midway.org).

91 Sunny Jim's Sea Cave

Pirate booty and slippery steps

Hidden in the back of a tiny, unassuming souvenir shop along Coast Boulevard in La Jolla is Sunny Jim's Sea Cave, a hand-dug tunnel down to the Pacific with a rather intriguing past.

In 1902, German artist and entrepreneur Gustav Schultz hired two Chinese laborers to carve out a tunnel from his house down to the cave, one of seven along La Jolla's cliffs. He wasn't the only local who wanted to do a little digging, however. Around the same time, a man named Thomas Diamond also petitioned to run a tunnel down from his property to the caves, along with one more tunnel under Cave Street that would connect all seven caverns. Diamond's request was ultimately denied, as many La Jolla residents were concerned about the destabilization of the bluffs that encompassed the caves.

After nearly two years, the work on Schultz's tunnel was completed, and visitors paid fifty cents each to make their way down to the cave. The trek was quite the feat at first, as the tunnel could only be descended on hands and knees – with a little help from some rope – until the steps were built several years later. But this didn't hold back the 200+ visitors per day.

One of the more well-known guests was L. Frank Baum, the author of *The Wonderful Wizard of Oz*, who is credited with naming the cave after he noticed that the entrance resembled the face shape of "Sunny Jim," a character that was used to promote Force, a British cereal in the early 1900s.

On a more scandalous note, the cave was allegedly used as a hideout by pirates, bootleggers, and human traffickers during prohibition, and rumor has it that the shop functioned as a speakeasy at one point. Fast-forward to present time, and the original 145 stairs are still in use, though at times they're a little slippery, so watch your step! The cave is as cool as ever – even without the secret speakeasy or lost pirate booty.

Address 1325 Coast Boulevard, La Jolla, CA 92037, +1 (858) 459-0746, www.cavestore.com, cavestore@gmail.com | Getting there Daily 9am–4:30pm | Hours Bus 30 to Pearl Street & La Jolla Boulevard | Tip Take a look from another perspective and explore the La Jolla caves from the outside in with a sea kayak tour from Bike & Kayak Tours (2158 Avenida de la Playa, www.bikeandkayaktours.com).

92 Surf Diva

Where everyone aspires to surf like a girl

Surf Diva in La Jolla Shores is an iconic surf shop and school that's been a place of empowerment and inclusion in the world of women's surfing since it was founded back in 1996 by twin sisters Coco and Izzy Tihanyi.

Coco and Izzy are more than just surf lovers – they're groundbreakers in the sport. They spent their early years riding waves, and Izzy became a competitive surfer during college. Both sisters have experience working in the surfing industry. They saw a huge gender gap in the world of surfing, with few opportunities for women to learn, compete, and excel. This realization was the driving force behind the creation of Surf Diva, where the mission is to provide a safe, supportive space for women in the traditionally male-dominated sport of surfing.

At the heart of Surf Diva is the highly respected surf school, which offers expert guidance for people of all ages, skill levels, and ability. It began as the first surf school for women and girls and became a co-ed one in 2002. With a team of skilled instructors, students receive individualized instruction to boost their confidence and skills while riding the waves. The consistent, beginner-friendly waves are just down the street from the shop, and they're perfect if you are just getting acquainted with a surfboard, or if you're looking for a bit more advanced instruction.

The shop itself has a great selection of surf wear, swimwear, and accessories that have made it a go-to place in La Jolla for surf fashion and gear. And they sell all kinds of boards! Everything from beginner boards to custom-shaped, locally made ones. Surf Diva has also created an enthusiastic community that nurtures surf enthusiasts of all kinds. The divas place a strong emphasis on environmental responsibility, so promote ocean conservation and sustainable surf practices among their students and the wider surfing community.

Address 2160 Avenida de la Playa, La Jolla, CA 92037, +1 (858) 454-8273, www.surfdiva.com, askadiva@surfdiva.com | Getting there Bus 30 to La Jolla Shores Drive & Paseo Dorado | Hours Shop: daily 8:30am–6:30pm; see website to book lessons and workshops | Tip Check the local schedule and head over to the La Jolla Tide Pools during low or minus tide for a look at the ocean's biodiversity (300 Coast Boulevard, La Jolla).

93_Surfing Madonna Mosaic

A saint shredding some gnar for a good cause

What's a piece of art without a little controversy? In North County's Encinitas, a vibrant mosaic of the Virgin of Guadalupe surfing a wave, known as the *Surfing Madonna*, was installed under a railway bridge in April 2011 by local artist Mark Patterson and his friend Bob Nichols. The blending of Catholic imagery with Southern California's surf culture, along with its accompanying message, "Save the Ocean," quickly caught the attention of both locals and visitors, igniting conversations about art, spirituality, and environmentalism.

Patterson, a former NASA engineer turned artist, originally installed the 10-by-10-foot mosaic in secret, without obtaining permission from the city. Though it became instantly popular with the public, city officials classified it as unauthorized and ordered its removal due to its location near the railroad tracks. After months of debate, the mosaic was carefully removed in June 2011, but Patterson worked with the city to find a new, permanent home for the piece. In 2013, the *Surfing Madonna* was reinstalled at its current location outside the Leucadia Pizza Encinitas.

Beyond its artistic significance, the *Surfing Madonna* sparked the creation of the Surfing Madonna Oceans Project, a nonprofit organization founded by Patterson. The organization focuses on ocean conservation, beach cleanups, and raising awareness about environmental issues.

Over the years, it has raised hundreds of thousands of dollars for marine protection efforts and community programs, and hosts events like the annual Surfing Madonna Beach Run, which raises funds for ocean-related causes and draws participants from across the region.

Patterson passed away in September 2023, and it was a significant loss for the community. His legacy lives on, however, through the Surfing Madonna Oceans Project, which continues to advocate for the causes he cared deeply about.

Address Leucadia Pizza, 315 South Coast Highway 101, Encinitas, CA 92024, +1 (760) 917-5291, www.surfingmadonna.org, mike@surfingmadonna.org | Getting there Coaster to Encinitas; bus 101 to Encinitas Boulevard & Vulcan Avenue | Hours Unrestricted | Tip The 1883 Schoolhouse is now the home of the Encinitas Historical Society, where you can visit the one-room schoolhouse and learn how Encinitas has changed over the years (390 West F Street, www.encinitashistoricalsociety.org).

94_Tahiti Felix's Master Tattoo Parlor & Museum

The oldest tattoo parlor west of the Mississippi

The artists at Tahiti Felix's Master Tattoo Parlor & Museum have been tattooing San Diegans since 1949, making it the oldest tattoo shop on the West Coast. It is located in the Gaslamp Quarter, but it hasn't always been there. Over the years, Tahiti Felix's moved through seven locations before landing here on 5th Avenue.

The shop was founded by "Tahiti" Felix Lynch, whose life was as colorful as his work. After stowing away on a ship as a young man, Felix ended up in Tahiti, where he married his wife, Nui, and embraced the beauty of Polynesian culture. Upon returning to the US, Lynch learned how to tattoo at Long Beach's famous Pike shop and went on to open his own place in San Diego.

Today, Gil Taimana, whose sister married one of Felix's sons, is the third owner of the shop. Born in Tahiti and raised in LA, he works alongside a team of full-time artists and also hosts guest tattooers from around the world for a mix of experience and fresh ideas.

The shop specializes in traditional Americana tattoos: bold, clean designs like anchors, eagles, and pin-up girls. These timeless styles are a big part of the shop's legacy, though the artists here are also known for creating custom tattoos in a wide range of styles.

People like Jerry Garcia and members of the notorious Hells Angels have been tattooed here. It's clearly the place to go for some fresh ink that'll leave a lasting impression.

Even if you're not in the market to get a tattoo, the shop houses a museum featuring vintage tattoo flash (designs that are ready to be tattooed right away) from the 1930s to 1960s, old tattoo machines, and other memorabilia. It's a space in which you can spend a ton of time just taking in the different styles and appreciating the artistry, whether you decide to take the plunge or not.

Address 924 5th Avenue, San Diego, CA 92101, +1 (619) 239-2684, www.mastertattoo.com, mastertattoo1949usa@gmail.com | Getting there Bus 215, 225, 235, 280 or 290 to Broadway & 5th Avenue | Hours Mon, Tue, Thu, Fri, Sat noon–6pm | Tip Take a look at more historical flash tattoo art from around the world, including rare art from the 1960s and '70s at The Arcade (604 Mission Avenue, Oceanside, www.arcadetattoo.com).

95 Taylor Guitars Tours

A look into where the magic happens

Founded in 1974 by Bob Taylor and Kurt Listug, Taylor Guitars has grown from humble beginnings into an industry favorite, revered for its innovation, precision craftsmanship, and commitment to sustainability.

These guitars, known for their bright, clear tones and exceptional playability, are favored by musicians across genres, from Taylor Swift to Jason Mraz. Legends like Prince, Neil Young, and Zac Brown have also counted on Taylor's instruments to deliver their signature sound on some of the world's biggest stages.

For those who want to check it out firsthand, Taylor Guitars offers free guided tours of their El Cajon factory. The tour begins with the selection and cutting of raw tonewoods; everything from Hawaiian Koa to Neo-Tropical Mahogany. Visitors then go through each stage of the guitar-making process, learning how precise, computer-aided machines shape the wood, while expert hands add the finishing touches.

One of the best parts of the tour is its focus on Taylor's innovative designs, which have set new standards in the guitar industry. Guests can observe up close as master luthiers assemble each guitar, meticulously sanding, shaping, and polishing the instruments to perfection.

As the tour goes on, Taylor's sustainability practices take center stage. From the reforestation efforts in Cameroon, to the use of urban woods that would otherwise go to waste, visitors get to see how environmental responsibility is crucial to the company's operations.

The final part of the tour shows how each guitar undergoes a rigorous quality check to ensure it delivers the signature Taylor sound. Watching the techs string and tune the guitars gives visitors a firsthand sense of the care and precision that goes into every instrument; whether guitar-obsessed, or mildly interested, you're bound to gain a deep appreciation for the work it takes to make a Taylor guitar.

Address 1980 Gillespie Way, El Cajon, CA 92020, +1 (619) 258-1207, www.taylorguitars.com, support@taylorguitars.com | Getting there By car, take CA-125 N to exit 20B and turn left on Grossmont College Drive. Turn left onto Fanita Drive, right onto Weld Boulevard, and right onto Gillespie Way. The destination is on the west side of the road. | Hours Visitor center Mon–Fri 9:30am–4pm; tours must be booked in advance online | Tip Keep the musical vibe going and book an appointment to check out the Deering Banjo showroom (3733 Kenora Drive, Spring Valley, www.deeringbanjos.com).

96 Thomas "Peg Leg" Smith

A larger-than-life liar

Thomas Long Smith, better known as Peg Leg Smith (1801–1866), is quite the character in the story of the American frontier. He lost his leg in 1827 during a fur-trapping expedition. Despite this setback, he continued his wild lifestyle, often using his wooden leg as a weapon in fights.

Smith was a one-legged mountain man, fur trapper, gold prospector, and a famous character of the Wild West. He was also involved in the darker side of frontier life. He enslaved American Indian children and sold them for labor on *haciendas* in Mexico. Then he turned to horse thievery.

In 1829, while passing through Borrego Springs, Smith allegedly discovered pure gold (initially mistaken for regular stones) in the area. He buried the rocks but was never able to relocate the treasure. This tale of lost gold, known as "The Lost Pegleg Mine," became a legendary story, attracting numerous prospectors hoping to find the elusive riches. Peg Leg capitalized on the legend by selling maps to the supposed location of the gold, although no one ever found it.

The Peg Leg Smith Monument, a seemingly unremarkable pile of rocks, commemorates Smith. In 1947, artist Harry Oliver erected a sign near the monument instructing visitors to "add 10 rocks to this pile" if they sought Peg Leg's gold. Over time, this tradition has resulted in a substantial pile of stones. The site was designated a California Historical Landmark in 1960.

Now, of course, not all of this is left in the past. Every first Saturday in April, the Annual Peg Leg Smith Liar's Contest is held at the monument, and storytellers from all over gather to share tales about the Old West and the legendary Peg Leg Smith.

Fun tidbit: Peg Leg Smith also appears in the 1995 computer game *Oregon Trail II*, where players can interact with him and purchase supplies from his post, adding another layer to his enduring legacy.

Address 2356-2408 Henderson Canyon Road, Borrego Springs, CA 92004, www.hmdb.org/m.asp?m=51585 | Getting there By car from the Borrego Springs Welcome Center, head south on Stirrup Road toward Palm Canyon Drive, and turn left at the first cross street onto Palm Canyon Drive. Continue onto Pegleg Road, turn left to stay on Pegleg Road, and continue onto Henderson Canyon Road. The monument will be on your right. | Hours Unrestricted | Tip Head to the nearby Clark Dry Lake, which has been used for everything from homesteading cattle to World War II bombing to low frequency radio astronomy research. Underneath the stunning, crackled lakebed, however, are brine shrimp and spadefoot toads waiting for the rain to fall (Rockhouse Trail/Rockhouse Drive, Borrego Springs, www.borregoexperience.com/clark-dry-lake-loop).

97_Torr Kaelan Building

The exemplification of beauty and sustainability

In the middle of San Diego's East Village, the Torr Kaelan building is a fascinating structure to look at, but it's also an experience and a must-visit for those intrigued by the fusion of modern architecture and sustainable living. Crafted by architect Rob Wellington Quigley, this five-story, mixed-use edifice is a paradigm of how buildings can harmoniously blend into their urban environment while championing zero-energy living.

What distinguishes Torr Kaelan from its neighbors is its embodiment of sustainable design in every aspect. Its white concrete façade is visually striking and pays homage to environmental consciousness in urban architecture. The building's orientation and materials reflect a deep understanding of how structures can minimize their ecological footprint while also maximizing functionality and aesthetic appeal. The blend of residential spaces and the Quigley Architects offices within the building breaks conventional architectural norms by presenting a unique live/work concept that's both innovative and practical, especially at a time when working from home is often the norm.

For design and art lovers, the interaction of light and shadow across the building's surfaces, the intelligent use of space, and the fluid transition between indoors and outdoors are beyond aesthetically pleasing, and all speak of Quigley's architectural prowess. It's an immersion into a vision of what modern urban living can be: sustainable, elegant, and seamlessly integrated with its surroundings.

For architecture enthusiasts and casual observers alike, make the time to take a long look at this building. It's an opportunity to witness how innovative design can transform the way we think about and interact with our urban spaces, beautifully capturing the concept of sustainable architecture and creativity within San Diego's urban landscape.

Address 416 13th Street, San Diego, CA 92101, +1 (619) 232-0888, site.robquigley.com, office@robquigley.com | Getting there Trolley to Park & Market (Blue, Orange or Silver Lines); bus 12, 901 or 929 to 10th & Island Avenues, or bus 3 or 5 to Market Street & Park Boulevard | Hours Viewable from the outside only | Tip Fan of stunning architecture? Head to Congregation Beth El to see a beautiful mixture of Eastern and Western architecture bathed in natural light (8660 Gilman Drive, La Jolla, www.cbe.org).

98 The Torrey Pine

A rare, resilient species

Torrey Pines State Reserve is arguably one of the most beautiful spots in San Diego. The views are stunning, the spring blooms rival those of the desert, and its hiking trails are a favorite for people of all ages. What makes it extra special, however, is its namesake tree: the Torrey Pine.

Named after the American botanist John Torrey (1796–1873), this pine species is native to just two restricted areas: Soledad Valley and Santa Rosa Island. Most of these rare trees find sanctuary within Torrey Pines State Reserve, which was established in 1959 to protect their dwindling populations.

The tree, while considered critically endangered, has some special survival strategies that have protected it from extinction thus far. Its extensive root system anchors it firmly in the sandy bluffs, enabling it to withstand the coastal winds that buffet its habitat. The unique shape of the pine's branches creates a canopy that captures the morning fog, causing water droplets to fall from them, a process known as "fog drip." This moisture provides a vital water source in the arid coastal environment, sustaining the tree and its surrounding ecosystem.

However, factors like drought, pollution, and invasive bark beetles contribute to its ever-dwindling population. The trees also need the help of birds and rodents to disperse the seeds and ensure the continuation of the species, unlike most pines, which rely on the wind.

Thankfully, Torrey Pines State Reserve serves as a haven for these rare trees and the diverse wildlife around them. The park offers opportunities for visitors to observe the Torrey Pine and its unique surroundings by trekking through the extensive network of trails that wind through coastal scrub habitat. Or, for an even more in-depth connection to the trees, the reserve also offers weekly guided Mindful Walks, led by knowledgeable docents.

Address 12600 North Torrey Pines Road, La Jolla, CA 92037, +1 (858) 755-2063, www.torreypine.org, contact@torreypine.org | **Getting there** Bus 101 to North Torrey Pines Road & State Beach. Walk down N Torrey Pines Road, turn right onto N Torrey Pines Park Road, and continue till you reach the Visitor Center. | **Hours** Daily 7:15am–dusk; see website for Visitor Center hours and guided hike times | **Tip** Visit the *Sunset Seat* and admire the view from atop this bench/sculpture, with a carved red-tailed hawk, made from a dead Torrey Pine (130-210 S Camino Del Mar, Del Mar).

99_Total Raptor Experience

Learn an ancient skill, with a view

Sure, hanging out at Torrey Pines Gliderport is an adventure for those keen to soar above the ocean, but it can be an even more unique encounter with the help of the Total Raptor Experience, a falconry school that's been running on site since 2014. Over the years, it's offered a glimpse into the ancient art of falconry, which dates back to 1700 BCE, allowing nature enthusiasts to engage with majestic falcons and learn about the birds' roles in both the ecosystem and human history.

The sport of falconry originated hundreds of years ago in the Far East as a means of hunting wild game for food. It was more of a survival skill than a sport at that time, though it was practiced even by nobility and seen as a status symbol. The art was passed down from generation to generation, and it was often taught to the sons of upper-class men just like other skills, such as archery or horseback riding. Both in the past and now, the highlight of the sport is the deep bond and trust that's formed between the falconer and the bird – a relationship that's central to the success of falconry.

The Total Raptor Experience brings this ancient tradition to the modern world, as participants step into the shoes of these historic falconers. They get to connect with a part of history that's been intertwined with nature for centuries and enjoy the thrill of calling a falcon to their gloved hand, feeling its power as it swoops over the bluffs. Each 90- to 120-minute Falcon Flight Encounter delves into the birds' lives, exploring their flight patterns, and conservation. The incredible views from the edge of the cliffs at the gliderport are a magnificent bonus.

Another bonus, your signed waiver allows you to enjoy the space after the experience, so take some time to enjoy the beauty and solitude of the cordoned-off area and watch the hang-gliders, paragliders, dolphins, and whales do their thing.

Address 2800 Torrey Pines Scenic Drive, La Jolla, CA 92037, www.totalraptorexperience.com, info@totalraptorexperience.com | Getting there By car, take I-5 to exit 29 and turn right onto Genesee Avenue, then left onto N Torrey Pines Road. Turn right onto Torrey Pines Scenic Drive. | Hours By appointment only | Tip Pack a picnic and take in the sunset on the cliffs above Black's Beach, just south of the gliderport (La Jolla, www.flytorrey.com).

100 The Twin Inn

An architectural, storied legacy

Smack dab in the heart of Carlsbad stands the historic Twin Inn, a beautiful building that's much more than eye candy. What stands today represents the area's rich history, beginning in the late 1800s with the establishment of a grand hotel near the mineral-rich well that drew settlers to the area.

Originally built to cater to travelers seeking respite and rejuvenation, the hotel soon found itself in the middle of a thriving community. In a stroke of architectural symmetry, two magnificent Queen Anne-style homes were erected on the same block, each a mirror image of the other. Gerhard Schutte, a Civil War veteran and president of the land company, led the construction of one home, while his partner, D. D. Wadsworth, oversaw the creation of the identical counterpart.

The glory, however, was short lived. Following a fire that razed the hotel in 1886, the two homes, left standing side by side with the hotel no longer there, took on a new role. Dubbed the Twin Inns, they offered lodging and meals to travelers passing through. Over the decades, the Twin Inns witnessed transformations and renovations, each adding to their charm. The addition of a rotunda in 1922 and a lobby remodel in 1936 further enhanced the appeal, drawing admiration from locals and visitors alike.

One of the most intriguing chapters in the Inns' history, however, unfolded during Prohibition, when a speakeasy operated in the basement, catering to folks seeking a taste of forbidden libations away from prying eyes. The bar attracted people from near and far, including some Hollywood stars looking for a little excitement.

One of the Inns was torn down in 1950, leaving behind a singular legacy – the mansion that had belonged to Schutte. Today, the remaining building is a cherished landmark, housing a variety of businesses, including a board shop, an electric bike company, and a publishing house.

Address 2978 Carlsbad Boulevard, Carlsbad, CA 92008 | Getting there Coaster to Carlsbad Village; bus 101 to Carlsbad Boulevard & Oak Avenue, or bus 315 or 325 to Carlsbad Village | Hours Unrestricted | Tip Visit the nearby, year-round State Street Farmers Market for locally grown fresh produce and unique artisan goods (2907 State Street, Carlsbad, www.carlsbad-village.com).

101_Ulysses S. Grant Portrait

A timeless nod to the former president

Opened in 1910 by Ulysses S. Grant Jr. (1852–1929), son of the famed 18th president of the United States, the US Grant Hotel was envisioned as a grand symbol of San Diego's growing stature. Its Beaux-Arts architecture and opulent interiors quickly made it the city's premier destination for dignitaries, socialites, and travelers seeking luxury in Southern California in the early 20th century.

Today, upon walking into the lobby from the main entrance, you'll find the portrait of Ulysses S. Grant displayed under spotlights, surrounded by framed mirrors. Painted by Urban Lawrence Gray (1876–1962), the piece captures the quiet strength and dignity of the former president. Gray, known for his detailed and classical portrait style, created the artwork with a sense of admiration for the legacy of the man who helped reunite a fractured nation. The portrait, with its fine brushwork and deep, commanding tones, is not only a decorative piece of art, but also a constant reminder of the hotel's origins, tied to the Grant family's aspirations and the symbolic weight of their name.

Urban Lawrence Gray, though not widely known beyond his time, was a master at conveying character through his work. His ability to capture the stoic resolve of Ulysses S. Grant is evident in every stroke. This portrait, one of Gray's most recognizable works, is one of the hotel's ways of preserving its historical legacy, reminding all who pass through those doors of the story behind the hotel.

Beyond this titular portrait, the US Grant Hotel has an impressive collection of original artworks, valued at $6.5 million. The artworks are curated to reflect the cultural and historical richness of the region, from contemporary Native American pieces, an homage to the Sycuan Band of the Kumeyaay Nation that now owns the hotel, to classic works that highlight the elegance of early 20th-century America.

Address 326 Broadway, San Diego, CA 92101, +1 (619) 232-3121, www.marriott.com/en-us/hotels/sanlc-the-us-grant-a-luxury-collection-hotel-san-diego | Getting there Trolley to Civic Center (Blue, Orange or Silver Lines); Surfliner to Santa Fe Depot; bus 2, 7, 110, 901, 932, 929 or 992 to Broadway & 3rd Avenue | Hours Unrestricted | Tip While at the Grant, grab a bite at the Grant Grill and learn all about the "men only" policy from the mid-1900s, and how and when the rules were changed (326 Broadway, www.grantgrill.com).

102 USS *Recruit*

The ship that never sailed

As a Navy town, San Diego has no shortage of ships. One of the coolest ones, however, is landlocked. Often referred to as the "USS Neversail," the USS *Recruit* training ship was commissioned in 1949 as part of the Naval Training Center (NTC) to provide hands-on training for new recruits. While it never touched the ocean, the *Recruit* was an essential part of the Navy's training program, simulating life aboard a ship for more than 50,000 sailors between 1949 and 1989. It continued to act as a training ship until the NTC closed in 1997.

The *Recruit* is a two-thirds-scale model of a destroyer escort, built from sheet metal over a wood frame on a concrete slab, complete with bridges, radar systems, and deck fittings designed to replicate the experience of a real Navy vessel. In 1982, it was reconditioned to resemble a modern, guided-missile frigate, but its function remained the same: to teach recruits about ship operations without ever leaving shore. While it's a bit of an odd sight (just a casual Navy ship next to a Hilton Hotel), the *Recruit* was once a vital training tool, giving sailors practical experience in navigation, gunnery, and ship duties.

After the base closed, Liberty Station was redeveloped into a cultural and commercial space packed with restaurants, shops, art galleries, and parks. The USS *Recruit* still stands there, a reminder of the area's naval past, its presence offering a stark contrast to lively, modern businesses surrounding it. That said, it's not just taking up space at Liberty Station. While it's no longer an active training tool, it's now open to the public on weekends, offering visitors a chance to step aboard and explore its history. Inside the *Recruit*, you can view old photos and detailed ship information, and get a deeper look at naval life and training from a time when San Diego's naval operations were at their height.

Address 2558 Laning Road, San Diego, CA 92016, +1 (619) 756-7992, libertystation.com/go/uss-recruit, info@libertystation.com | Getting there Bus 923 to the N Harbor Drive & Laning Road | Hours Sat & Sun noon–4pm; unrestricted from the outside | Tip While at Liberty Station, grab a cozy table for two in a vintage red Fiat and share an authentic, Neapolitan-style pizza at Officine Buona Forchetta (2865 Sims Road, www.officinebuonaforchetta.com).

103_Villa Montezuma

San Diego's mystical mansion

Villa Montezuma is an incredibly preserved example of Victorian-era architecture, tucked away in San Diego's Sherman Heights neighborhood. The former home of musician Jesse Shepard was added to the National Register of Historic Places in 1971.

Shepard (1848–1927) was no ordinary performer. Originally from the United Kingdom, he used the pen name Francis Grierson and was known for his vast piano skills and extraordinary vocal range. He claimed to channel the spirits of composers like Beethoven and Chopin during his performances. His concerts, around both Europe and the US, were part musical performance, part spiritual experience. Shepard arrived in San Diego at the urging of a pair of real estate developers, the High brothers, who coaxed him to the area to create a "Palace of the Arts." He wanted to build a home that reflected his artistic and mystical ambitions, and that is when Villa Montezuma was born.

Designed in the American Queen Anne style, the mansion is an architectural marvel. It features stained-glass windows, intricate woodwork, and a grand piano room where Shepard held private concerts. Completed in 1887, the mansion's gothic towers and ornate interiors created an atmosphere where the supernatural seemed almost palpable. Shepard believed the house itself enhanced his spiritual connection to the great composers, and guests often reported feeling an otherworldly presence during his performances.

Despite the spectacular performances, Shepard's stay in San Diego was brief, as financial problems forced him to leave just a few years after the house was completed. Even so, Villa Montezuma became a symbol of artistic expression and mysticism in the city. Today, the mansion is preserved as a museum, and you can enjoy going on tours offered most weekends, which provide a glimpse into Shepard's world and the unique architecture of the building.

Address 1925 K Street, San Diego, CA 92102, +1 (619) 233-8833, www.villamontezumamuseum.org, fovm@villamontezumamuseum.org | Getting there Bus 4 to Imperial Avenue & 19th Street | Hours Tours Fri–Sun, by appointment only | Tip Take a walk through Bankers Hill, home to about 50 Victorian-style homes, notably the H. H. Timken House (2508 First Avenue), Long-Waterman House (2408 First Avenue), and the Britt-Scripps Manor (506 Maple Street).

104_Washington Street Skatepark

A grassroots park for the pros

There's no doubt that San Diego has a solid skate culture. After all, it's home to one of the first skateparks in the world, it's where the first laminated board was made, and some of the best skaters out there, including Tony Hawk, Shaun White, and Patti McGee, hail from here. So it's no surprise that the city hosts one of the very best skateparks around.

Nestled under the expansive stretch of the Pacific Highway, just minutes from the airport and Little Italy, is the Washington Street Skatepark. Built in 1999 during a time when the city's skaters were seeking refuge from a downtown skateboarding ban and a lack of public skate spaces, this park was designed, funded, and created by skaters for skaters. It has played a pivotal role in the sport.

The concrete curves and ramps of this old-school skate haven are ingeniously tucked under a freeway, providing shelter from the sun and allowing the park and its surroundings to blend seamlessly. From the smooth bowls to the challenging lines and over-vert capsule, each feature was designed to push the limits of skateboarding. There is also a variety of beautiful murals and mosaics spread throughout the park, adding to the community feel of the place.

This no-frills, skate-only zone, where bikes, scooters, and roller-blades are a strict no-no, has become hallowed ground for the skate-boarding elite. Don't be surprised if you find yourself sharing the ramps (or, more likely, watching the ramps) with pro skaters, who often drop by to test their mettle against some of Southern California's most challenging features.

For the non-skater, Washington Street Skatepark offers a spectacle like no other. Spend an afternoon here, and you'll be treated to a display of some of the most skilled skateboarding in the country.

Address Pacific Highway & Washington Street, San Diego, CA 92110 | Getting there Trolley to Washington Street (Blue or Green Lines); bus 10 to Washington Street & Trolley Tracks | Hours Mon 9am–5pm, Tue–Thu & Sun 9am–7pm, Fri & Sat 9am–5pm | Tip Check out Slappy's Garage for all kinds of skateboards and accessories, along with in-house, screen-printed shop gear (two locations: 465 17th Street & 6585 Osler Street, www.slappysgaragesd.com).

105 The Whaley House

Hauntings and history abound

Right in the heart of Old Town lies a historic gem shrouded in eerie legends and captivating tales. The Whaley House, a Greek Revival-style mansion, was designed and built in 1857 by Thomas Whaley (1823–1890) and his family, who were early San Diego settlers. Their home offers a blend of history and the supernatural.

The Whaley House has been many things over the years: a residence, a general store, a courthouse (the second in San Diego County), and even a theater. Since it was first built, however, there have been a variety of tragedies that led to its reputation as one of the most haunted places in the country.

Sightings of apparitions believed to be members of the Whaley family are among the most common occurrences. Witnesses describe glimpses of Thomas Whaley, his wife Anna, and their daughter Violet, appearing as if they're living out their daily routines within the walls of the house. Other former occupants of the home, like Thomas Tanner, who operated the theater but died in the house just 17 days after opening, have also been seen.

It's not just visions, however, that visitors have experienced. There have been claims of unexplained sounds, sudden drops in temperature, unidentified touches from unseen hands, and an eerie sensation of being watched, even when alone in a room. For those with a keen nose, the scent of lavender is said to occasionally fill the air (Anna was known to have a love for lavender).

While the authenticity of these ghostly tales remains up for debate, a visit to the Whaley House is the only way to decide for yourself just how haunted it is – or isn't. Self-guided day tours and guided night tours are offered, and there's also an After-Hours Paranormal Investigation Tour that includes the use of ghost-hunting equipment, giving visitors the best chance of coming across something a little spooky.

Address 2476 San Diego Avenue, San Diego, CA 92110, +1 (619) 273-5824, www.whaleyhousesandiego.com | Getting there Trolley to Old Town Transit Center (Blue or Green Lines); bus 83 to Juan & Harney Streets, or bus 83 or 105 to Old Town Transit Center | Hours See website for tours and schedule; reservations recommended | Tip Head just up the hill to the Witches Tower at Presidio Park to see where the first American was buried in California. It's said to be quite haunted (2752 Presidio Drive).

106_Whiskers & Wine

A purrfect lounge experience

Step into Whiskers & Wine and enter a feline paradise. You'll find the cozy atmosphere of a cat café with the unique twist of a kitchen serving up delectable bites (like the "Pawsitively French" flatbread or "Italian Cat Grass Salad") and creative cocktails (like "Whiskey Meower" or a "Meownhattan") from their fully licensed bar. Here, amidst the comforting hum of conversations and delicate purrs, you'll find yourself in a delightful realm where cats reign supreme (obviously).

First and foremost, Whiskers & Wine is thoughtfully designed with its feline residents in mind; fun hidey-holes, tunnels, things to scratch and climb, and a special cat staircase create a playful and engaging environment for both the cats and their human guests.

Visitors aged 12 and above are welcome, and reservations are a must. This approach ensures that neither the kitties nor their human visitors feel overwhelmed, allowing for plenty of quality time to interact and bond. The space is layered, allowing guests to move between the main and second levels, each offering a different ambiance to suit whatever they're in the mood for. The upper level also has a great airflow, so those worried about dander can breathe a little easier.

Naturally, one of the best parts about this spot are the weekend kitten yoga sessions, which take place almost every Saturday and Sunday. Although there's no guarantee of one-on-one time with a kitty, when they do choose to join in, their cuddles eclipse the importance of yoga poses. It's a reminder that in this space, the cats set the pace and the agenda (again, obviously).

Fun and cuteness aside, most of the kitties are adoptable, though there are some resident ones, and the incredible staff at Whiskers & Wine are dedicated to providing a comfortable, safe space for the sweet little creatures looking for their forever homes.

Address 2856 Adams Avenue, San Diego, CA 92116, +1 (619) 837-2325, www.whiskersandwinebar.com, info@whiskersandwinebar.com | Getting there Bus 11 to Adams Avenue & Utah Street | Hours Tue–Thu 4–8:15pm, Fri 4–9:45pm, Sat 10am–9:45pm, Sun 10am–6:45pm | Tip Enjoy another four-legged yoga experience at Blackledge Farms' goat yoga sessions (2377 San Vicente Road, Ramona, www.blackledgefarms.com).

107_White Labs Brewing Co.

Where beer nerds and science geeks collide

Merging science with delicious brews, White Labs has crafted a unique space in San Diego's bustling beer community as a brewery, a yeast laboratory, and a place of learning for decades. Located aptly on Candida Street, White Labs, the brainchild of Chris White, PhD, has been demonstrating the intricate dance between fermentation and yeast since 1995.

From its early days, White Labs earned its reputation as a yeast-production powerhouse, even predating the brewery's launch. As a pioneer in yeast science, it's subtly influenced numerous iconic brews worldwide by offering an expansive selection of premium yeast strains. The laboratory is a paradise for microbial aficionados (aka "germ nerds"). Here, yeast strains are meticulously crafted, preserved, and studied, ensuring each strain retains unparalleled purity, resulting in consistently exceptional brewing outcomes.

Education is a priority for White Labs. Through courses and workshops both in-person and online, it imparts knowledge to homebrewers and professionals alike, spanning topics from yeast management and foundational fermentation to advanced brewing strategies. Its commitment to education fosters an ever-evolving brewing standard that benefits both brewers and drinkers.

Within the taproom, guests also get to experience the transformative power of yeast! By using a single base recipe and altering only the yeast variety, the brews showcase a spectrum of flavors, emphasizing just how pivotal yeast is to the final taste profile. A side-by-side tasting of these beers provides customers with a really unique and enlightening perspective on the unsung hero of brewing.

Science, innovation, and brewing genius aside, White Labs also offers an excellent space to kick back, enjoy a pint, and indulge in delicious bites, many of which owe their flavors to the very yeast created within these walls.

Address 9495 Candida Street, San Diego, CA 92126, +1 (858) 527-7362, www.whitelabsbrewingco.com, info@whitelabs.com | Getting there Bus 31 to Black Mountain & Carroll Center Roads | Hours Tue–Thu 2–8pm, Fri noon–9pm, Sat & Sun noon–8pm | Tip Spend a post-beer afternoon at nearby Lake Miramar and rent a rowboat or paddleboat from the concession (10710 Scripps Lake Drive, www.rockymountainrec.com/lake-facilities/listing/lake-miramar).

108_ WorldBeat Center

A celebration of cultures

As you step into the WorldBeat Center, the energy is palpable. The walls are adorned with vibrant art pieces, and flags of different nations hang from the ceiling. This spot is so much more than a showcase of cultures. It's a living celebration and preservation of the African diaspora and Indigenous cultures, welcoming visitors to witness diverse traditions and fully immerse themselves in a world of rhythmic beats, vivid colors, and spirited dances.

At the helm is Makeda "Dread" Cheatom, the visionary founder who has transformed the WorldBeat Center into a thriving community space where education, understanding, and unity flourish. The Center's impact extends far beyond its physical boundaries, reaching schools and local organizations through extensive outreach programs and spreading a message of peace and cultural appreciation.

What sets the center apart is its authenticity, as it breathes life into cultures by encouraging visitors to participate rather than simply observing. Every hosted event or class (think pulsating Middle Eastern drumming workshops, smooth belly dancing, and lively samba classes) promises an authentic experience. It's a wonderful venue for performances, and it's a gateway to understanding and appreciating the world's diverse heritage through the universal language of art and music. Another standout part of the center is its EthnoBotany Peace Garden. The purpose of the garden is to teach people of all ages and backgrounds about the role of plants and the relationship between plants and people, and to address the issues of food and water crises in San Diego.

In a city synonymous with sunshine and surf, the WorldBeat Center offers a different kind of escape, one that travels the globe without ever leaving San Diego. Regardless of whether you're a local or a tourist, a visit promises a unique journey into the heart of global culture.

Address 2100 Park Boulevard, San Diego, CA 92101, +1 (619) 230-1190, www.worldbeatcenter.org | Getting there Bus 7 or 215 to Park Boulevard & Inspiration Point Way | Hours See website for center and café hours and events | Tip Also in Balboa Park is the Centro Cultural de la Raza, a center dedicated to celebrating and preserving Chicano, Latino, Mexican, and Indigenous art and culture (2004 Park Boulevard, www.centrodelaraza.com).

109_The World's Biggest Lemon

A sweet slice of Lemon Grove history

If you've ever ridden the Orange Line trolley through Lemon Grove, chances are you've seen the town's most beloved landmark: a 10-foot-long lemon sculpture that has been standing proudly for almost a century. It's hard to miss – it's huge, it's bright yellow, and it sits right by the tracks with the slogan, "Best Climate on Earth." While the lemon makes for a quirky photo op, its representation of the town's citrus heritage and love of community make it really special.

The story of the Giant Lemon goes all the way back to 1928, when the Lemon Grove Chamber of Commerce decided to show off its town's agricultural roots in a big way. The job of designing the lemon fell to Alberto Treganza (1876–1944), a local architect and artist whose family was deeply connected to the area. But this couldn't just be any oversized fruit, and Treganza had a method. He asked local lemon growers to submit their finest specimens, carefully chose a final 12, and then selected the perfect lemon on which to base the sculpture.

When it was time to build, a group of local ranchers brought the design to life. Led by local grower and contractor Edmund J. Dunn, who planted his orchard in the 1920s and whose trees still thrive today, the group assembled the big lemon with timber, chicken wire, plaster, and paint. It came together just in time for the 1928 Fiesta de San Diego parade, where Treganza's daughter, Amorita, rode atop it as the very first Miss Lemon Grove. The float was a hit, appearing in parades for several years until 1932, when the residents of Lemon Grove couldn't bear to part with it. Thanks to local businessman Tony Sonka, who paid to have it permanently mounted on a plinth in front of his general store, the *Giant Lemon* found its forever home. It's been sitting near the railroad tracks ever since, only moving a little bit over the years to make room for rail lines.

Address 7777 Broadway, Lemon Grove, CA 91945 | Getting there Trolley to Lemon Grove Depot (Orange Line); bus 856 or 936 to Broadway & Buena Vista Avenue | Hours Unrestricted | Tip Peruse the well-stocked – and well-priced – wares at the Lemon Grove Antique Mall (7919 Broadway, www.lgantiques.com).

110_ZLAC

Rowing tradition lives on, one stroke at a time

On the edge of Mission Bay is ZLAC Rowing Club – a "blink and you might miss it" kind of spot with a story that stretches back more than 130 years. Established in 1892, ZLAC is the oldest women's rowing club in the world and a piece of living history that still thrives today.

Founded by four young women, Zulette Lamb and sisters Lena, Agnes, and Caroline Polhamus (hence, the acronym), the club started out as a small group of members rowing wooden barges from a boathouse on Market Street. It has evolved into a fixture of San Diego's rowing scene, moving to its current Mission Bay location in 1932. While many women's rowing clubs sprouted across the US in the early 20th century, ZLAC is the only original one still going strong.

The clubhouse was designed by famed local architect Lilian Rice (1889–1938), who also served as ZLAC's president in the early days. The understated gardens that surround it were designed by Kate Sessions (1857–1940), also known as the "Mother of Balboa Park."

ZLAC may be private, with membership offered by invitation only, but it isn't just for insiders. The club opens its doors to anyone who wants to learn the sport with Learn-to-Row classes for women of all ages. Once you've completed the introductory class, you can join ZLAC's rowing programs, even if you're not a member.

Now, let's be honest. Rowing is no small feat. It's a full-body workout that engages about 85% of your muscles. It also happens to be something that a lot of people are into. ZLAC has about 400 members, ranging in age from teens to women in their 90s, many of whom have been rowing for decades! Some ZLAC rowers have gone on to compete at the highest levels, but plenty of others just row for the love of it. Regardless of your rowing aspirations, take a class or two not just for fun, but to participate in and contribute to something historical.

Address 1111 Pacific Beach Drive, San Diego, CA 92109, +1 (858) 274-0661, www.zlac.org, info@zlac.org | Getting there Bus 8 or 30 to Grand Avenue & Cass Street, or bus 9 to Ingraham Street & Fortuna Avenue | Hours See website for class schedule and rowing program | Tip Take a more chill approach to spending time on the water with food stations and bottomless mimosas on a Champagne Brunch Cruise (990 N Harbor Drive, flagshipsd.com/cruises/brunch-cruise).

111__Zoro Garden

From nudist colony to butterfly haven

Within the heart of Balboa Park is the Zoro Garden, a serene escape into nature. What few realize, however, is that this tranquil butterfly garden has a colorful, controversial past.

Architect Richard Requa (1881–1941) originally conceived the space for the 1935 California Pacific International Exposition. He designed a sunken stone grotto and garden packed with lush plants and flowing water features. The intended use of this oasis-like environment was beyond the public's wildest imagination (drumroll, please): a nudist colony exhibit!

It was a daring concept. Visitors flocked to see paid performers who hailed from nature cults around the US and even Switzerland, who lived out their daily routines in the garden – completely in the nude. The goal was to offer an anthropological glimpse into the nudist lifestyle, highlighting the health benefits of sunbathing and natural living, and, naturally, to provide a bit of shock value.

Marked as an educational exhibit, it quickly became one of the exposition's most controversial attractions. It drew large crowds, but also faced sharp criticism from conservatives, who deemed it indecent and scandalous, sparking heated debates about propriety and public morality.

Visitors to the gardens during the exposition saw the performers engaging in a variety of activities, from sunbathing and exercise to communal games and "body beautiful" contests. The scheduled shows and demonstrations added to the allure (and controversy) and proved irresistible to curious audiences.

When the exposition ended, so did the nudist colony. It was dismantled and repurposed into a public space, which still thrives today. Now a butterfly garden, it's a haven for the winged creatures, featuring nectar plants, host plants, and shelters to support the butterfly lifestyle – a lifestyle very different from the space's originally intended one.

Address El Prado, San Diego, CA 92101, balboapark.org/parks-trails-gardens/zoro-garden-balboa-park | Getting there Bus 7 to Park Boulevard & Village Place | Hours Unrestricted | Tip Feel like getting naked? Gladiator Beach at the edge of San Onofre State Beach is clothing optional (Old Pacific Highway, south of San Onofre Trail 6, Agra).

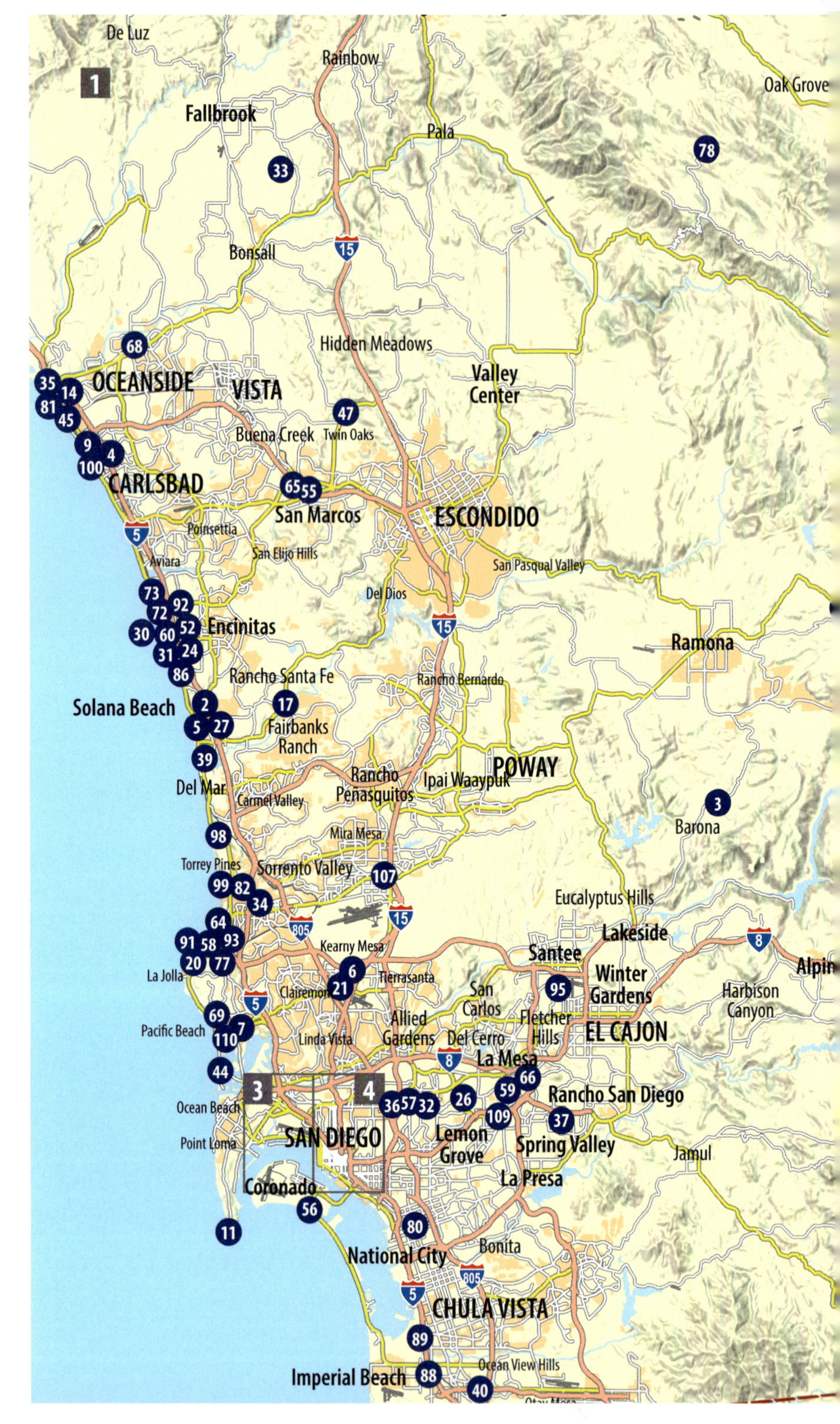
1
De Luz
Rainbow
Oak Grove
Fallbrook
Pala
78
33
Bonsall
15
Hidden Meadows
68
35
14
OCEANSIDE
VISTA
Valley
Center
81
45
47
Buena Creek
Twin Oaks
9
4
100
CARLSBAD
65
55
San Marcos
ESCONDIDO
5
Poinsettia
San Elijo Hills
Aviara
San Pasqual Valley
73
92
Del Dios
72
Encinitas
30
60
52
15
31
24
Ramona
86
Rancho Santa Fe
Rancho Bernardo
Solana Beach
2
17
5
27
Fairbanks
Ranch
39
POWAY
Rancho
Peñasquitos
Ipai Waaypuk
Del Mar
Carmel Valley
3
Barona
98
Mira Mesa
Torrey Pines
Sorrento Valley
107
99
82
34
Eucalyptus Hills
15
64
805
91
58
93
Kearny Mesa
Lakeside
8
Santee
20
77
La Jolla
6
Tierrasanta
Winter
Gardens
Alpin
21
Clairemont
San
Carlos
95
Harbison
Canyon
5
69
Allied
Gardens
Fletcher
Hills
EL CAJON
Pacific Beach
7
110
Linda Vista
Del Cerro
8
La Mesa
44
66
3
4
59
Rancho San Diego
Ocean Beach
36
57
32
26
109
37
SAN DIEGO
Lemon
Grove
Point Loma
Spring Valley
Jamul
Coronado
La Presa
56
11
80
Bonita
National City
805
5
CHULA VISTA
89
Ocean View Hills
Imperial Beach
88
40

2
Warner Springs
96
12
42
Borrego Springs
13
28
Julian
Viejas
8
8
54
Campo
Tecate
USA
MEXICO
N
0
2.8 mi

3
Sea World Drive
San Diego River
Ocean Beach Freeway
Taylor Street
Mission Valley Freeway
Hancock Street
Juan Street
Fort Stockton Drive
Congress Street
Old Town
Mission Hills
Sports Arena Boulevard
105
76
29
Sunset Boulevard
Midway Drive
San Diego Avenue
Evergreen Street
Barnett Avenue
84
Lytton Street
Locust Street
41
Pacific Highway
Kite Street
104
51
Willow Street
Rosecrans Street
Truxtun Road
Midway Avenue
85
1
Neville Road
Historic Decatur Road
Guantanamo Street
Cushing Road
San Diego International Airport
Laning Road
North Harbor Drive
15
102
Harbor Island Drive
San Diego Bay
49
Murray Street
Moffett Road
Saufley Street
4th Street
2nd Street
Quentin Roosevelt Boulevard
Stockdale Boulevard
N
0
0.2 mi

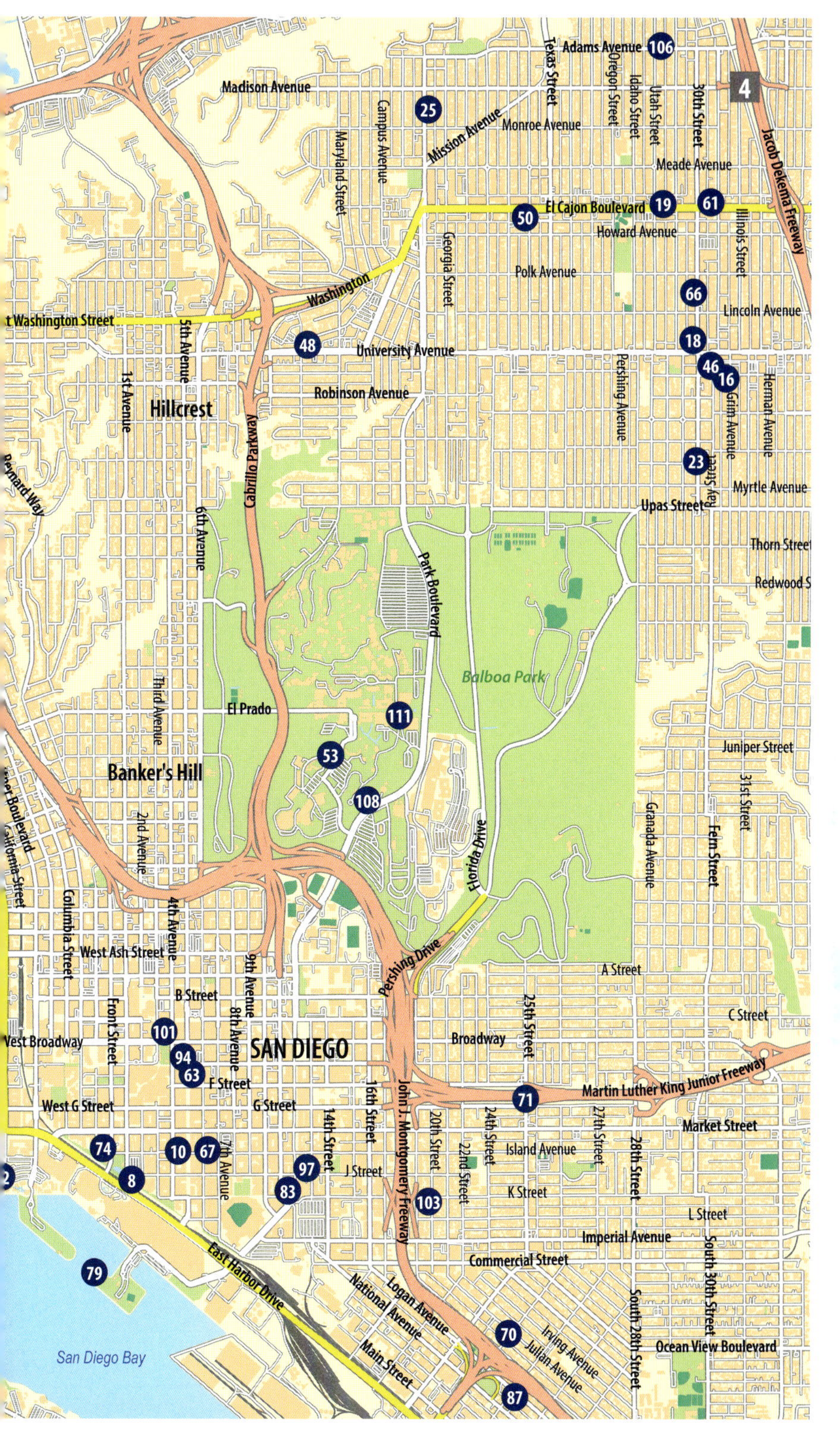

4
Adams Avenue
106
Texas Street
Oregon Street
Idaho Street
Utah Street
30th Street
Madison Avenue
25
Campus Avenue
Maryland Street
Mission Avenue
Monroe Avenue
Meade Avenue
Jacob Dekema Freeway
El Cajon Boulevard
19
61
50
Howard Avenue
Georgia Street
Illinois Street
Polk Avenue
Washington
Washington Street
66
Lincoln Avenue
5th Avenue
48
18
University Avenue
46
16
Robinson Avenue
Pershing Avenue
Grim Avenue
Herman Avenue
1st Avenue
Hillcrest
Cabrillo Parkway
23
Myrtle Avenue
Upas Street
6th Avenue
Park Boulevard
Thorn Street
Redwood S
Balboa Park
Third Avenue
El Prado
111
Juniper Street
53
Banker's Hill
2nd Avenue
108
Granada Avenue
31st Street
Fern Street
Florida Drive
Columbia Street
4th Avenue
West Ash Street
Pershing Drive
A Street
9th Avenue
B Street
8th Avenue
C Street
Front Street
25th Street
101
Broadway
West Broadway
94
SAN DIEGO
63
F Street
Martin Luther King Junior Freeway
71
West G Street
G Street
16th Street
John J. Montgomery Freeway
20th Street
24th Street
27th Street
Market Street
14th Street
Island Avenue
74
10
67
7th Avenue
22nd Street
28th Street
97
J Street
8
83
103
K Street
L Street
Imperial Avenue
South 30th Street
79
East Harbor Drive
Commercial Street
Logan Avenue
National Avenue
South 28th Street
70
Irving Avenue
Julian Avenue
Ocean View Boulevard
San Diego Bay
Main Street
87

Laurel Moglen, Julia Posey, Lyudmila Zotova
111 Places in Los Angeles That You Must Not Miss
ISBN 978-3-7408-1889-0

Brian Joseph
111 Places in Hollywood That You Must Not Miss
ISBN 978-3-7408-1819-7

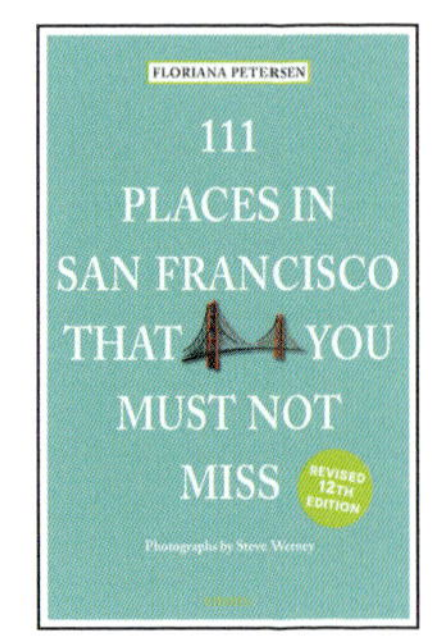

Floriana Petersen, Steve Werney
111 Places in San Francisco That You Must Not Miss
ISBN 978-3-7408-2058-9

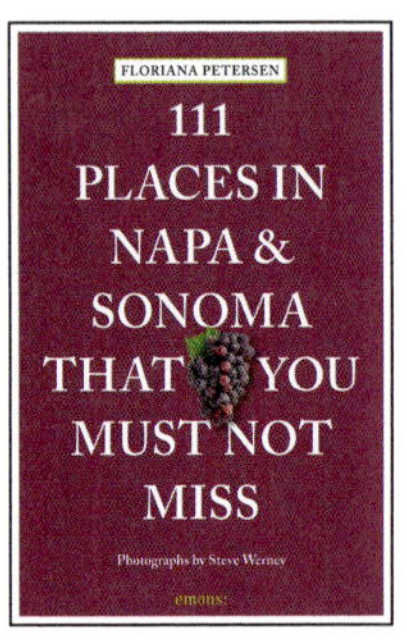

Floriana Petersen, Steve Werney
111 Places in Napa and Sonoma That You Must Not Miss
ISBN 978-3-7408-1553-0

Floriana Petersen, Steve Werney
111 Places in Silicon Valley That You Must Not Miss
ISBN 978-3-7408-1346-8

Travis Swann Taylor
111 Places in Phoenix That You Must Not Miss
ISBN 978-3-7408-2050-3

Philip D. Armour, Susie Inverso
111 Places in Denver That You Must Not Miss
ISBN 978-3-7408-1220-1

Dana DuTerroil, Joni Fincham, Daniel Jackson
111 Places in Houston That You Must Not Miss
ISBN 978-3-7408-2265-1

Dana DuTerroil, Joni Fincham, Sara S. Murphy
111 Places for Kids in Houston That You Must Not Miss
ISBN 978-3-7408-2267-5

Kelsey Roslin, Nic Yeager, Jesse Pitzler
111 Places in Austin That You Must Not Miss
ISBN 978-3-7408-1642-1

Travis Swann Taylor
111 Places in Atlanta That You Must Not Miss
ISBN 978-3-7408-1887-6

Susan Veness, Simon Veness, Kayla Smith
111 Places in Orlando That You Must Not Miss
ISBN 978-3-7408-1900-2

Cristyle Egitto, Jakob Takos
111 Places in Palm Beach That You Must Not Miss
ISBN 978-3-7408-2398-6

John Tucker, Ashley Tucker
111 Places in Richmond That You Must Not Miss
ISBN 978-3-7408-2002-2

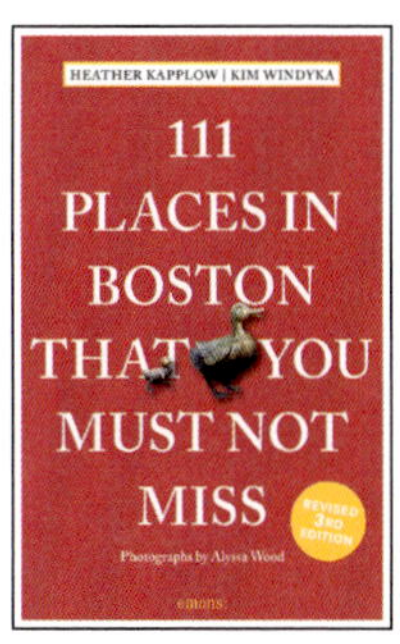

Kim Windyka, Heather Kapplow, Alyssa Wood
111 Places in Boston That You Must Not Miss
ISBN 978-3-7408-2056-5

Jo-Anne Elikann, Susan Lusk
111 Places in New York That You Must Not Miss
ISBN 978-3-7408-2400-6

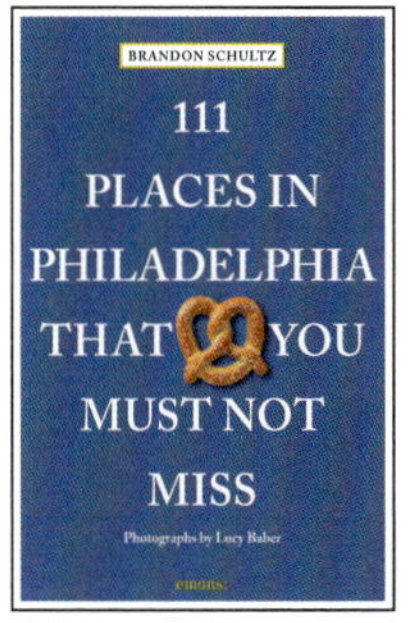

Brandon Schultz, Lucy Baber
111 Places in Philadelphia That You Must Not Miss
ISBN 978-3-7408-1376-5

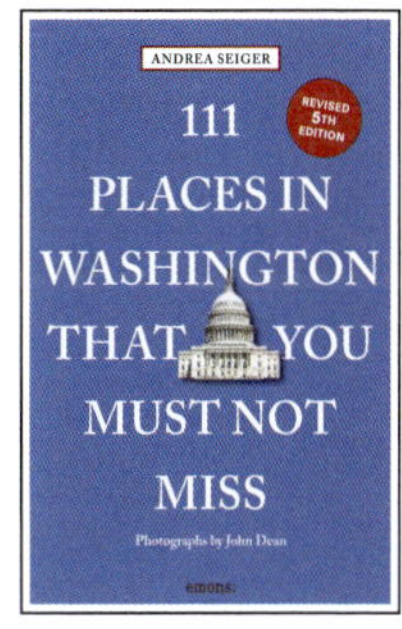

Andrea Seiger, John Dean
111 Places in Washington That You Must Not Miss
ISBN 978-3-7408-2399-3

Thank you, Chris, for being my home, for always being supportive of my dreams, no matter how ridiculous they are (yes, I still want to start a pickle company, have a farm – despite my lack of a green thumb or talent – and own a coffee shop / wine bar / bookstore / general rom-com situation that belongs in a Hallmark movie), and for forcing me to travel when we were oh-so young. (Don't worry, readers! It wasn't an "I need to be rescued by Liam Neeson in *Taken*" kind of thing – he just always pushes me to conquer my fears.) You made me look at, capture, and share my experiences of the world in a different way. Your help and patience throughout this process is single-handedly what got me through the times when I didn't think I could do it.

Thank you, Molly the pup, you are my heart, and thank you for teaching me it's okay to be an introvert – life is always great when snuggling up with you, a cozy blanket, and a good book – but also for reminding me that it's important to step out of my comfort zone and wag my proverbial tail.

Thank you to my parents, for always believing in me, no matter what, and for truly being the most generous, open-hearted, humble people I've ever met (and I met you like, right away, so that's pretty impressive). Thank you, Ali, for being my constant inspiration in both creativity and kindness. You make me want to continuously evolve and believe in myself. To my San Diego fam, thank you for being you – your energy and ridiculousness bring so much joy and make me want to experience life (and share it through my words and photos) to the fullest.

Writing and photographing a book has been a dream of mine for years, and this entire experience has been both challenging and rewarding. I especially want to thank Karen Seiger, my editor, for taking me on. I am so grateful you took a chance on me and trusted me with this venture. To Emons Verlag, the publishing team that made all of this happen, I am beyond grateful for all your hard work and for transforming all of my raw materials into something beautiful.

Most importantly, thank you San Diego, for truly being one of the most incredible places on earth. Your culture, beauty, people, and food and drink scene are remarkable, and it has been such an honor to be able to share some of it with my readers.

Photo Credits

Barona Cultural Center (ch. 3): Courtesy of Barona Cultural Center & Museum; Belly Up (ch. 5): Courtesy of Belly Up; Diversionary Theatre (ch. 25): Simpatika; Fallen Star (ch. 34): Philipp Scholz Rittermann; The Giant Dipper (ch. 44): Courtesy of Belmont Park; Gossip Grill (ch. 48): Photos by Brittany Leach; Mujeres Brew House (ch. 70): Vito Di Stefano; Rady Shell Open Rehearsals (ch. 79): Courtesy of San Diego Symphony; San Diego Central Library (ch. 83): Rob Wellington Quigley; San Diego Circus Center (ch. 84): Jean-Luc Martin; The Self-Realization Fellowship (ch. 86): Courtesy of Self-Realization Fellowship, Los Angeles, California; Surf Diva (ch. 92): ©surfdiva.com; Torr Kaelan Building (ch. 97): Darren Bradley

Art Credits

Greatest Generation Walk (ch. 49): Seward Johnson, *Unconditional Surrender*, edition IV/VI, 2013, cast bronze, 300 x 156 x 156 inches, © 2004, 2005 The Seward Johnson Atelier, Inc.
https://sewardjohnsonatelier.org

Stephanie Arsenault is a freelance writer and photographer specializing in food and travel. Originally from Canada, she now resides in Oceanside, California. When she's not taking photos or writing, Stephanie can be found making beautiful baked goods in her sunny kitchen or hanging out on a nearby patio with her husband and pup, and a local beer in hand.

The information in this book was accurate at the time of publication, but it can change at any time. Please confirm the details for the places you're planning to visit before you head out on your adventures.